Orlando Diaz-Azcuy

# Orlando Diaz-Azcuy

## by Diane Dorrans Saeks

RIZZOLI
NEW YORK

Previous Page: For a San Francisco Decorator Show-case, an annual fundraiser for San Francisco's University High School, Orlando Diaz-Azcuy created the dramatic dining room. His challenge was to design around an immovable object—a nine-foot-diameter dining table that was designed by Michael Taylor in travertine marble. (The house would later be for sale, and the table would be among its intact contents.) The designer fought back by circling the table with eight of his teak indoor-outdoor Portico tables designed for McGuire, here stained a handsome ebony and upholstered in tan leather. A grisaille wallpaper panel made its first appearance in his design lexicon and was later featured in his Manhattan apartment. The silver torchères were designed by Diaz-Azcuy for Boyd. To further tame the table, he hung a cone of light from the ceiling and planted a circular tray of fresh grass on top. Curtains are Calvin silk.

Above: In an Edwardian house in San Francisco, Orlando Diaz-Azcuy placed a graphic sculpture by Harry Bertoia on a gilded marble-top Italian table, showing each to advantage. "Rooms always benefit from the contrast of antique and modern, refined and rough, and rococo and contemporary," says the designer.

# Contents

# Foreword
## by John Saladino

Orlando Diaz-Azcuy is a friend and an admired colleague. I met him in San Francisco long ago at a design conference. He was simply and eloquently attired in elegant white linen summer clothing.

In the times we have met since then, I have always noted the modernity and clarity of his appearance. His very presence is a signature of his design philosophy. His work, like him, is always beautifully groomed. He is a protégé and also a protagonist in the minimalist aesthetic, and a fellow principal who also creates timeless design spaces.

Orlando's residential and commercial work of the last four decades is a seamless mastery of scale, proportion, and color. A sense of calm pervades all his interiors. His immaculate attention to the geometrical shapes of the selected furnishings suggests elegant dancers in a ballet. The work is always a professionally edited environment in which the very air seems calculated and weighed in the balance of design. Viewing his oeuvre is an extreme pleasure and nurtures one's sense of optimism, clarity, and order. Orlando's work always offers a vision of what a better world can be.

*Opposite:* New York designer John Saladino has commented that "good design is exaggeration" and that "the classical world is the well from which I drink every day." His concept for the sumptuous dining room at the Italianate villa Las Tejas in Santa Barbara reflects his romantic approach to interiors. Like Orlando Diaz-Azcuy, who also looks to design history for inspiration, Saladino uses icons like urns and columns to add nobility, grandeur and a sense of history to rooms.

# Into the Light
## by Diane Dorrans Saeks

For his clients, Orlando Diaz-Azcuy custom-designs opulent chairs and sofas, and seeks out rare art and graceful and dramatic antiques from the best international antiquaires and galleries. For himself, he spends years, even decades, stalking recherché antiques, fine authentic George III gilded chairs, contemporary paintings and sculptures by new artists, and out-of-print architecture and design books.

But the fastidious Mr. Diaz-Azcuy knows that fine and eccentric design is also to be found in the dusty haunts of Paris flea markets and Camden dealers. He may find a dazzling treasure *chez* Axel Vervoordt in Antwerp, or he may take a walk on the wild side and go junking in San Francisco's Mission district. Gritty Valencia Street or obscure corners of Manhattan can be great places to stalk antiques, according to the cashmere-clad designer. Expressive and lasting design is found in precisely this high/low mix.

Orlando Diaz-Azcuy, an award-winning designer of furniture, textiles, lighting, and interiors, has been based in San Francisco for the last forty-five years and also operates a design office in Manhattan. He founded his eighteen-person firm Orlando Diaz-Azcuy Designs in 1987, after working for more than twelve years as a design principal

*Opposite:* In the dining room of his St. Francis Wood house, Diaz-Azcuy juxtaposed the perfect poise of two square-backed antique gilded chairs with a sleek, oval marble-topped Saarinen table, one of eleven Saarinen tables of various dimensions he has collected. His new Boyd chandelier floats below the ceiling in sculptural contrast to the rough-hewn beams. Also in elegant opposition: the sleek Saarinen table on the sawn and adzed floors, and a pair of simple gilded mirrors above two gessoed, fluted urns. The timber door and window grille are original to the Spanish Colonial–style house.

for Gensler, the international architectural firm, also based in San Francisco. His company is now named ODA Design Associates, with principals David Oldroyd and Greg Stewart, who both joined the firm within months of its founding.

In addition to a design portfolio of private residences around the world, Diaz-Azcuy's firm has completed designs for the spa at Hong Kong's Peninsula Hotel, the chic "Intermezzo" patrons' lounge at the San Francisco Opera house, law offices in London, athletic clubs in Northern California, a Los Angeles cancer center, restaurants, investment banking centers, and hotels in Japan and Thailand. His present and past clients include such manufacturing companies as McGuire, Steelcase, Stow Davis, Schumacher, Hickory Business Furniture, Boyd Lighting, and Pallas Textiles.

As a modernist, Mr. Diaz-Azcuy is a secret romantic. His interior architecture tends to be minimally detailed, but in the luxurious textiles and colors he selects, there is always a touch of va-va-voom. Modernist living rooms he limns are jolted with sensual lavender silk velvets, acid-green silk taffeta, Fortuny's shimmering gilded fabrics, and a retinue of contemporary paintings and sculptures.

"I am always battling design conservatism and clients' perpetual longing for the familiar," he says. "I like to stretch myself and my clients as far as possible. They are starting to really appreciate modernism and admire minimalism."

Diaz-Azcuy has designed best-selling teak collections for McGuire, as well as a powder-coated aluminum collection. His Versailles-inspired indoor-outdoor teak furniture, saber-legged tables, classically inspired rattan chairs, and dark-stained maple tables for McGuire have been wildly successful and emulated.

## A CUBAN CHILDHOOD—INTERRUPTED

Some of Orlando Diaz-Azcuy's ambition and fire doubtless comes from his dramatic early life. The son of a Cola-Cola distributor in Pinar del Río, he enjoyed an idyllic childhood in small-town Cuba—until Fidel Castro brought an end to it.

"I grew up in a typical, simple stucco house with a tile roof, an interior courtyard, and with a certain formality and discipline imposed by both parents," he recalls. "Cuban houses in smaller towns were just a white cube with perhaps one touch of exuberant color and a chandelier. This controlled color palette, this concern for the minutest detail of design and the splash of color, have played out in all of my designs. I have never liked excess. I like simplicity with a touch of glamour."

His elder brother bought him a subscription to *House Beautiful*, and at the age of nineteen Diaz-Azcuy persuaded his mother to paint the living room flamingo pink.

"Havana at that time was very cosmopolitan, and my college student accommodations there were in a very grand Beaux-Arts inspired building," he notes. "There were also Richard Neutra houses built in Cuba. It was a stimulating atmosphere for a young design aficionado." Cuba at that time had world-class musicians and ballet dancers, and a lively art scene, he recalls.

In 1962, at a time when Cuban politics were at a boil, Diaz-Azcuy was sent by his family to study architecture at Catholic University in Washington, D.C.

"I didn't really speak English then at all, and I got through lectures and studies phonetically with help from fellow students," he said.

Upon graduation, Mr. Diaz-Azcuy acquired a Volkswagen Beetle and headed west. He went on to complete a master's degree in landscape architecture and city and regional planning from the University of California at Berkeley.

Diaz-Azcuy does not dwell on what his life might have been had he not escaped to Miami.

"I left Cuba for ideological reasons, and I have never been back," says Diaz-Azcuy. "I still have a haunting image of what it used to be and the beauty that is gone forever. But I don't look back. Never."

## DISCIPLINED DESIGNER

"My Cuban side would have me dancing all night, going to a show, studying, working, all in a continuum with lots of social time with my family and friends every day," says Diaz-Azcuy. "But I don't live that way. My life has always been focused on what will make me happy. Design and my design studio and working on new projects are always fulfilling for me."

His design colleagues usually see only this studious side, he says.

"I probably seem very serious, a bit formal, a bit boring, and maybe a little arrogant," Diaz-Azcuy says. "Some

*Opposite:* For an apartment overlooking Central Park, Diaz-Azcuy opened rooms and left windows bare of curtains so that the expansive views could be enjoyed from every corner. Sunlight is modulated with MechoShades. The dining table was designed by Diaz-Azcuy. Chairs, by Patrick Naggar, are from Ralph Pucci.

potential clients think I'm going to be very expensive and only interested in luxurious things. But that's a misconception. I am a perfectionist, but extravagance is not one of my weaknesses when I am working with my clients."

Diaz-Azcuy, who has an all-white design studio on Post Street in downtown San Francisco, recently moved into a glamorous penthouse in Pacific Heights. He keeps a high-rise apartment and office in New York and is decorating a new Miami apartment.

"I lead a very simple, unpretentious life; my holidays and my travel are focused on design and art and architecture," says Diaz-Azcuy. "I love to spend time at home reading political exposés and books on antiques and art. I try to work at home on Fridays. I love the solitude. It's a day for me and my brain. I need to be alone. It's peaceful for me—and essential."

Diaz-Azcuy travels often—to Tokyo, Los Angeles, Paris, Venice, Antwerp, New York, Miami, London, Berlin, Nice, Barcelona, and Florence—and always with a design agenda.

"I plan my life a lot, and that includes my vacations," he says. "Nothing is left to chance. I see my life clearly. I have been very fortunate to be in the right place at the right time—and I have been ready to seize all of these great opportunities."

## STYLE AND SERENDIPITY

If Diaz-Azcuy has ever had a disappointment, a tepidly received furniture collection, a downturn in business, or any serious reverse in the upward trajectory of his career, and indeed in his life story, it is difficult to find one.

When asked if he has ever had a grand reversal or regret, Mr. Diaz-Azcuy gives an almost apologetic grin and shakes his head thoughtfully.

"I have been incredibly lucky in my life, and I have always worked hard," he explaines. In his personal life, too, he has been blessed. He has shared his life with John Capo, a former design showroom manager, since 1966.

The designer enjoys the challenge of working on intense projects in California and New York City.

"It's not a stretch or a dramatic change for me to be working in New York," Mr Diaz-Azcuy says. "I have always had clients here, and have spent a great deal of time working on apartments on Park Avenue, and Central Park South."

"New York is very different from California," he admits. "There's a difference in the scale of rooms and furniture, and the practical issue that everything in New York has to be able to fit into an elevator, or be dismantled and reassembled. I've never been known for overscale, giant furniture anyway."

Diaz-Azcuy is now embarking on a new series of furniture designs for McGuire, along with a rigorous series of international projects for longtime clients.

To explain his continuing success, Diaz-Azcuy notes his work ethic.

"Although Cuba was in a period of dramatic change, I have been very disciplined since I was five," he says. "My parents were disciplined people, and everything in my family home was structured and ordered, in the best manner. I work well in a structured environment with everything well planned. I'm flexible but organized. I like to spend time working on problems. I arrange my life to be very productive. I enjoy life on my own terms. I don't believe in excess or wasting time. I put my work out there, with no compromise."

Diaz-Azcuy also points out his way of working with clients.

"I've become adept at explaining the pragmatic part of design to my clients and clarifying all issues," he says. "I explain the logical reasons for design decisions. It is not about 'taste' or emotion. Most successful designers know how to explain very rationally. I look at each project with a fresh eye and open mind. Experience gives you an advantage, but you must be open to every new challenge. Once you start repeating yourself, with interiors or furniture, you've lost the edge. You must keep creating, exploring new ideas, taking risks."

Asked what has powered him and ignited his passion for design over almost five decades, Diaz-Azcuy notes his search for emotional satisfaction, never at anyone else's expense.

"It's perfection and purity that drive me," he says. "If I am not pleased with my design, it's not worth it. For me it comes down to the project. Is it worthwhile? Can something of great quality be achieved? Perfectionism drives me crazy because there is always some degree of compromise to do with money, time, reality. Some clients confuse my drive for

*Opposite:* In a Russian Hill apartment, Diaz-Azcuy turned a former closet into a romantic media room. A Fortuny-covered banquette is arranged with a collection of superb gold-printed velvet and silk pillows by Sabina Fay Braxton and custom-made chenille bolsters. The television is wall-mounted and pivots.

perfection with ego. It's not. I know what's best and what's appropriate. A room has to feel right, and it has to function. It's profound, and I want the perfect solution. Some people may say, 'That's arrogant,' so I have always tempered what I say. But I will say, I know how to solve a problem."

Diaz-Azcuy believes that lasting interior design cannot be about style alone. The day-to-day work can no longer simply be a choice between being a modernist or creating traditional design.

"Projects must be about what you want to accomplish for your client and yourself," he says. "This is custom design. In the end, both the client and the designer must be satisfied. Designers must create work that satisfies their standards, and it should be the perfect fit for the client, in every sense."

## A STUDY IN WHITE

In his three downtown San Francisco design studios, the designer has made a point of creating calm, orderly workplaces.

"For me and my staff, it's a laboratory for developing ideas," he says. "The environment, including the lab coats my colleagues and I wear, is white. It is very calm. You are not distracted, and your mind is clear. Floors are pale oak planks, carpets are pale ivory, and we display some antiques and sculptures. Walls have no trim. I did not want to present a specific style. The total concentration is on the clients' projects, not the décor."

As the owner and designer of sequential residences on both coasts, Diaz-Azcuy enjoys experimenting and expressing new ideas, free of clients' constraints.

"I had so much satisfaction designing my first little house, which I acquired in 1981," he says. "It was built in 1904, and was vaguely Victorian with a bay window in front. I lacquered the interior walls in pale celadon, left them bare, with no art, and bleached the floors. It was minimalist before minimalism. It was simple, very calm. I felt it had inner beauty. In the living room I mixed an eighteenth-century gilded Venetian sofa upholstered in gold silk and a pair of Brno chairs. I had a white Saarinen table. In the dining room I had six Louix XV chairs, cheap copies, that I lacquered white, with white muslin seats. When I punctuate interiors I use pieces that are very luxurious, or very pared-down. I never go for the middle ground."

His best clients, he says, are well-informed, enthusiastic, and engaged.

"Over the years, I've worked with several generations of clients, for whom I do many residences. We make a great team," the designer says. "Faced with a large problem, I study and think about every aspect before I offer my first solution. I never give off-the-cuff solutions. I work with the client. I never argue with the client. I don't fight with the client. I have my own vision but I don't present it all at once. That can be overwhelming for a client and confusing. I choose my battles and fight them one at a time."

With ongoing projects for McGuire, Diaz-Azcuy is thinking about new furniture designs and concepts.

"I am always researching and studying the market," he says. "There is the philosophy on the future and the philosophy of today. I design for the market. I'd love to have a call to design avant-garde furniture to show at the Milan fair but that has not happened so far. To design for the market, my work must appeal and work for the end user. It's not abstract or theoretical design. It's based on reality, here and now. It must be confortable, and it must work in a broad range of environments."

Diaz-Azcuy faces the future, a realist but always an optimist.

"I have always wanted to design a contemporary house from the ground up," he notes. "The goal would be to design a family house, not a museum piece, based on ideas that provoke me. I would like it to be very pure, but to express influences from art, opera, and design. It would not be a palace. In it I'd express the essential purity of my design, to please, stimulate and inspire my clients and give them a fulfilling, comfortable, and inspiring life."

*Opposite:* Orlando Diaz-Azcuy's penthouse on the top of a hill in Pacific Heights faces directly south, and offers views of San Francisco Bay to the east and the Pacific Ocean to the west. A wall of windows and sliding doors has been softened and shaded with billowing curtains of lightweight Irish linen. A pair of contemporary black granite sculptures from Japonesque, San Francisco, is displayed on the flamed slate floor. "The most successful design is a result of rigorous, disciplined editing. Successful interiors are always the result of taking out and not putting in more things," said the designer. Among his longtime passions: German white porcelain, and hammered silver and vermeil objects by Josef Hoffman. The Noguchi-esque coffee table is from Blackman Cruz, Los Angeles.

# Chapter One
# Diaz-Azcuy Residences

The most successful interior design is a result of rigorous, disciplined focus and editing. Simple and elegant interiors are created by taking out and not putting in more things.

—Orlando Diaz-Azcuy

# Pure Genius

**It's grand opera—at its most alluring. In his dramatic new Pacific Heights penthouse, designer Orlando Diaz-Azcuy simplified the original interior architecture to create a dynamic gallery for the crème de la crème of his art and antiques.**

Orlando Diaz-Azcuy is a passionate modernist at heart. So it's not surprising that after spending a decade in a stately and rambling 1920s Spanish Revival house in St. Francis Wood, a suburb of San Francisco, he became restless. He started hunting for a modern apartment closer to his downtown studio.

"I wanted an apartment in a contemporary building that was in the right location, and not far from my office," says the designer.

Diaz-Azcuy, who founded ODA Design Associates in 1987, works on a range of residential and commercial interiors. After forty years of designing interiors for his clients, the Cuban-born designer decided to create his dream interiors, more rigorous and pure than any he had approached previously.

"San Francisco is a challenging place for a modernist to find an apartment, as the city has only a handful of great contemporary apartment buildings, so I searched for more than two years," says Diaz-Azcuy.

"Finally I discovered this penthouse in Pacific Heights with ten-foot ceilings and views from the Pacific Ocean to the East Bay, and I bought it on the spot," said the designer.

A perfectionist, Diaz-Azcuy immediately planned a ceiling-to-floor redesign of his apartment, which is on the seventeenth floor of a 1960s building in Pacific Heights, near Lafayette Park.

"The apartment was a standard three bedroom, with lowered ceilings, and all chopped up into small rooms," recalls Diaz-Azcuy. Residences in the building face either

*Previous spread:* A 1950s glass-topped table in his Pacific Heights penthouse offers Diaz-Azcuy the opportunity to create tablescapes with Murano glass candlesticks, a glass bowl, and a corybantic bronze figure.

*Opposite:* White curtains float in the breeze along the new gallery Diaz-Azcuy created by extending room onto the formerly open terrace. A pair of contemporary sculptures from Japonesque is displayed on the flamed slate floor. The handcrafted 1930s black leather chair is by Danish designer Fritz Henningsen.

directly north to the gray swathe of the bay or south over rows of Victorian houses and distant hills iced with fog. While most San Franciscans set their hearts on a bay view (with the Golden Gate Bridge and Bay Bridge framing the image), Diaz-Azcuy preferred the sunny, south-facing cityscape.

Two years of remodeling involved banishing a series of small rooms and opening up the space.

"I didn't want the interior architecture to deny that it's in a high rise," he says. "My goal was to achieve a light, fresh-air, California feeling."

He stripped down the interior architecture to make it feel calm, very minimal. No baseboards, no trim, no moldings.

"But I have to have luxury, too," he notes. "That comes from the soaring spaces, the span of windows, and then the antiques and the art and sumptuous fabrics."

Walls throughout the apartment have been sprayed with eggshell-finish off-white paint for a smooth, brush-free effect. Mechanicals and wiring are concealed in sections of lowered ceilings that run along the hallway. He even minimized the doors by concealing frames in the walls.

Diaz-Azcuy extended his apartment five feet onto a former balcony, in the process adding 350 square feet.

"I really did not need a seven-foot-wide, seventy-foot-long open terrace in San Francisco," he says. "It is generally too cool or too windy at this height

to stand or sit on the balcony. I preferred to have seven feet added to my living room, dining room, and study."

A wall of glass windows and sliding doors runs along the south-facing apartment. The eastern edge is now reshaped into two bedrooms and a comfortable study. At the opposite end is a large living room adjacent to the dining room, and a long, broad hallway. A practical white kitchen is fitted into a corner near the front entrance.

Floors throughout the house are a soft pale blue-gray Blue Lagoon limestone with a flamed finish. The apartment has subfloor radiant heat.

"I am always tempted to see how simple I can make drywall look, and I am seldom tempted to embellish," says Diaz-Azcuy.

The spacious, open rooms are the ultimate thrill for a

modernist, and the interiors are dazzlingly edited. "I like a sense of voluptuousness," says Diaz-Azcuy. "I love the idea of monastic interiors, but the heart desires beautiful things to look at and touch. I believe in superb comfort. I have a great appetite for modern furniture, but I use it as an accent, with upholstered pieces to actually relax on."

All this simplicity makes a sumptuous background for his collections of art and antiques. Eccentricity, contrasts, and surprises in furniture and art are key to the designer's confident style.

In the living room, he combined a Roman-style daybed upholstered in silk velvet with a quirky black-lacquered art deco chair with ball feet (variously attributed to Elsie de Wolfe and Tony Duquette), as well as a narrow table made of petrified wood.

*Previous spread:* Diaz-Azcuy devised an open plan for his living room, adjoining dining room, and the sunlit gallery that runs along the south-facing apartment. Placed like sculpture, a 1950s steel-based coffee table from Blackman Cruz adds bold curves to a seating group delineated by a pair of columns. The banquette and wall are upholstered in fabric from Henry Calvin, San Francisco.

*Above and opposite:* The Josef Hoffmann hammered silver and vermeil pieces on the table are part of Diaz-Azcuy's museum-quality collection of Wiener Werkstätte designs. White wall sconces throughout the apartment are from Orlando Diaz-Azcuy's new lighting collection for San Francisco–based Boyd Lighting.

*Above:* In his white-walled dining room, Diaz-Azcuy turned up the color volume with a saffron-and-tangerine-colored silk taffeta tablecloth, topped with an alluring mix of pink and smoky topaz crystal glasses, and antique Venetian glass candlesticks. The silverware is from Gumps.

*Opposite:* A 1920s handcrafted silver wine bottle stopper is from Diaz-Azcuy's Josef Hoffmann collection. The room is animated by bravura prints in permanent pigment and acrylic by California artist Deborah Oropallo, from the Stephen Wirtz Gallery, San Francisco. The Macassar dining chairs, which date from the 1930s, were acquired from Alabaster, San Francisco.

In another corner, a pair of Mies van der Rohe tan leather tufted ottomans is lined up near a sculptural 1930 Fritz Henningsen leather-and-teak armchair.

For the dining room, Diaz-Azcuy designed a tablecloth of saffron and tangerine shot silk. Walls are animated with Deborah Oropallo works of art. Also displayed is Diaz-Azcuy's museum-quality collection of Josef Hoffmann Wiener Werkstätte hammered silver urns, vases, wine-bottle stoppers, bowls, and decorative objects.

Diaz-Azcuy said that even while growing up in western Cuba, he was tuned in to design and architecture.

"Havana in the sixties was very cosmopolitan, and my college student accommodations there were in an elegant Beaux Arts–inspired building," he notes. "There were Neutra houses built in Cuba. It was a very stimulating atmosphere for a young design aficionado."

This early passion for modernist simplicity, a carefully controlled color range, and his love of gilt and luxury, and a rigorously pared-down architecture have played out in all of his designs. Diaz-Azcuy says that while the florid architecture of Havana had its energy and appeal, he has never liked excess in interiors.

For the moment, the apartment is bliss for the designer.

"For my clients I can design any style of interiors

*Above and Opposite:* Diaz-Azcuy designed a versatile study/office/film-viewing room with barrel-back 1930s chairs, slate-colored wool carpet, and ebony-lacquered bookcases. The hand-carved table, above, is African. The pair of 1930s Parisian ceramic lamps on the hexagonal table, right, was acquired from Hedge, San Francisco.

*Opposite and above:* Tonalities of pale gray were selected for the bedroom of John Capo, Diaz-Azcuy's partner of forty years. The Agnona cashmere blanket is from Sue Fisher King, San Francisco. A collection of Capo's extensive and highly edited Berlin KPM porcelain pieces is presented on the specimen-marble top of the 1920s Belgian black-lacquered table. The pastel crayon portraits of Francis Bacon and David Hockney are from a series by Don Florence.

ranging from very traditional to lofts, country houses, a pied-à-terre, offices, a hotel—but for myself it's a modern approach," says the designer. "For now, I find these rooms restful, calm, and personal, but I know the apartment will change and evolve."

"The daily hazard of being a decorator is that I am constantly exposed to the best art, amazing sculpture, the top collections, auctions, antiques, and accessories," says Diaz-Azcuy. "I buy pieces for their innate beauty, quality, and spirit. I know I'll see something exceptional at an auction or a gallery, an antiques shop or in a magazine. In six months, this apartment will look quite different."

*Above and opposite:* The décor of Orlando Diaz-Azcuy's bedroom has been kept somewhat spare and monochromatic, with just an antique Belgian verdure tapestry, a marble fragment from a Roman sculpture, and a series of antique terra cotta pottery silhouettes for contrast and texture. The designer prefers to keep clutter (and electronics) out of the bedroom, seeing it as a place for repose, contemplation, and peace and quiet.

# I'll Take Manhattan

**Police boats speeding up the East River, noble brick edifices on Beekman Place, and the sleek spires of mid-town are all in view from this privileged position.**

When he decided to open an office in Manhattan, Orlando Diaz-Azcuy began a search for an Upper East Side apartment with noble lineage. He hoped to uncover something fixable in a classic Park Avenue building.

Two years later, his pipe dreams went up in smoke, and he happily settled for a sun-filled 1,500-square-foot apartment on the twenty-third floor of a modern high-rise overlooking the East River and the gardens of the United Nations headquarters.

"I love the open uptown views, the bright light, the views of the river, and the true sense of being up in the sky," says the designer. "I can be at the theater in ten minutes. MoMA, or any antiques shop or gallery, is only a quick cab ride away. I am in the middle of everything, but the apartment is airy, quiet, and very private."

*Above and opposite:* For the first version (of many) of his Manhattan apartment, Diaz-Azcuy designed a bleached sycamore coffee table. Around it are a black-lacquered sofa and chairs, upholstered in Avanti wool from his collection for HBF Textiles. The pillows are also in his HBF Textiles designs. The wallpaper panel mounted on the wall is an eighteenth-century design depicting a Greco-Roman festival scene, possibly celebrating Juno.

*Previous spread:* The white table was designed by Diaz-Azcuy for McGuire. Above it hangs an eighteenth-century neo-Gothic Viennese carved and gilded chandelier. The floor is covered with limestone floor tiles. The lacquered cabinet, right, provides storage and conceals electronics.

*Opposite and below:* Newly installed mirrored panels double the apparent dimensions of the bedroom, which is furnished with a custom-designed daybed and a series of versatile cabinets. The daybed, crafted by Marco Fine Furniture in San Francisco, is upholstered in leather from S. H. Frank and wool twill by Henry Calvin. The pillows are in Calvin silks.

*Above:* When the renovation started, a gypsum board was removed from a weight-bearing concrete wall. Diaz-Azcuy decided to leave the pitted, stained, and rather Pompeian evidence just as it was—in juxtaposition to the sleek steel.

*Opposite:* Diaz-Azcuy ordered a precision-engineered and superbly elegant stainless-steel kitchen by Bulthaup. It is not that he is an enthusiastic cook, but an efficient and beautiful kitchen gives him enormous pleasure.

# A House in St. Francis Wood

**A rambling Spanish-style house with Pacific Ocean views offered the designer the opportunity to appoint traditional rooms with dramatic modern furniture of his own design.**

"I really wasn't looking for a traditional-styled house," avers Orlando Diaz-Azcuy. The designer, seeking simplification, had sold his Beaux Arts–style apartment on Russian Hill and had divested himself of his country cottage. For a time he entertained the idea of buying a modernist house, something more to his minimalist taste. Truly refined and elegant International Style houses are few and far between in San Francisco. The search proved not only disappointing but also fruitless.

Then Diaz-Azcuy was shown a 1938 Spanish Colonial–style house with possibilities—but with not a modernist inch to its architecture. The designer was immediately drawn to its beautiful siting on a slope with views of the bay and the ocean to the west. The house was elegantly arranged with a series of terraces featuring graceful stone arches, a sunny tiled loggia, ornate balconies, leaded glass windows, hardwood floors, and hand-plastered walls. Original ironwork grilles, light fixtures, and handsome door hardware added to its allure.

"I felt as if I were back in Cuba. It's just like the house I grew up in, in Havana," says the designer. He is not nostalgic for his homeland, but how could he resist?

The living room had eighteen-foot ceilings, with hand-carved beams and brackets said to have been salvaged from a fifteenth-century Spanish convent. Oak floors were adzed to look as if they were hand-sawn.

"It had never been remodeled," marvels Diaz-Azcuy. "For me the key was to keep the interiors simple and somewhat sparse. It's the architecture you should experience and enjoy, not a decorating statement."

*Opposite:* Silk taffeta pillows are piled on the linen slipcovered sofa in the living room. The floor lamp beside the windows is a Diaz-Azcuy design for Boyd Lighting, San Francisco. The white lacquered table was designed exclusively for HBF. Ceiling beams and carved corbels are original to the house. Sunlight from the west- and south-facing windows is filtered through simple linen curtains on iron rods.

*Opposite and above:* Diaz-Azcuy simplified the fireplace, replacing a dated ornamental mantel with a simple concrete design. In contrast to the painted Italian chairs and ornate iron chandelier, he placed his new, white lacquered table in the center of the room to energize what could easily have been an "homage to Spain" moment. Eclecticism is the designer's favored approach. "I never want to create a style you can name," he says. "It should be your style, not some preconceived notion or formula." Terra-cotta tiles and all stonework are original to the house.

*Above and opposite:* In the dining room, a Saarinen table is surrounded by George II gilded chairs with plain tacked muslin upholstery. Diaz-Azcuy designed the chandelier for Boyd Lighting. "I am a minimalist when it comes to architecture, but at the same time design is about life and day-to-day living, reading books, dining, gathering for a glass of wine, watching television, enjoying new acquisitions. I need to have beautiful things, surprising contrasts, richness and luxury, to live happily. I could not live in a monastic interior without antiques and art and modern pieces," he says. "I like voluptuous lighting and simple curtains that effectively manage the light. Chairs and sofas must be comfortable. Tables should be practical."

*Opposite and above:* In the taupe-walled study, Kraft paper–lined cabinet doors disguise electronic equipment and volumes on design and art. The terra-cotta tiled floor is original to the house. The tufted sofa, designed by Diaz-Azcuy, was covered in linen velvet, with chenille pillows. Four chairs from the HBF collection were slip-covered in natural unbleached linen, with a border in a Greek key pattern. The pendant lamps were improvised with Houlés jute tassels, a jute rope, and cheerful orange linen. The study, which opens to the loggia, is the ideal place in summer for cocktails before dinner on the terrace.

*Above and opposite:* While San Francisco is often foggy and windy in the summer, spring and fall are balmy and ideal for outdoor dining. The loggia, with graphic stone arches, makes an ideal staging point for flowers, but also works for a buffet or dinner party. The stone garden figures now stand in the lobby of the Post Street atelier.

*Following spread:* Diaz-Azcuy's ocean-view bedroom opens to a quiet terrace. He had the pristine, white-lacquered desk custom-made as both a work surface and for displaying his fine book collection. Concealed behind the smooth surface of the desk: drawers and shelves for sweaters, notebooks, and shoes. The designer wanted the simplest bed—really just a pencil sketch of a four-poster, with no embellishment or airs. He dressed it with an oversized cover made with yards of hemstitched, crunchy chartreuse silk taffeta from Silk Trading Co. The metal shapes on the desk were originally made in eighteenth-century Italy as models for aspiring artists to sketch and depict while learning shading and perspective.

*Above and opposite:* The guest bedroom is filled with light in the early morning. Natural linen draperies that fall perfectly with a slight "break" hang from simple wrought-iron rods. Diaz-Azcuy used plain fabrics throughout the house, so that drawing attention to the architectural details and perfect symmetry of the rooms would be evident.

# Russian Hill Residence

**In this dramatic departure from his all-white offices, the designer luxuriated in gilded antiques, down-filled sofas, and a silk-and-velvet-cocooned chinoiserie study.**

A 1913 Beaux Arts building with elaborate ironwork would hardly seem an obvious choice for a modernist designer who rips ornamentation off interiors without hesitation. However, the San Francisco Bay views, which included Alcatraz and Angel Island, and the sunny, south-facing bedrooms, were too compelling to resist.

"The building is elegant, and I appreciated the formality of the rooms, which are laid out on the north side in a classical enfilade," says Orlando Diaz-Azcuy. "The floor plan was perfect, so I did not touch a wall or make a single structural change. My concept was to make the rooms light, crisp, and classical."

Walls were painted in pale ivory shades, and hardwood floors were given a rich and glossy ebony finish. A custom-designed sofa filled with down and a series of deep-dish

*Above and opposite:* In the entry foyer, an eighteenth-century Venetian chair has a cartouche painted with a sweet-faced cherub. The cast-bronze bust, in the neo-classical style, is French, circa 1850. To the right is the dining room, and the door at left leads to the living room. Diaz-Azcuy also decorated the building's entry, with a marble-topped iron table of his own design and walls painted in tones of pale ochre.

club chairs added comfort to the living room. A large-scale black-and-white painting of two Korean sisters by Lordan Bunch adds a graphic punch to the monochromatic room.

The dining room (seldom used for formal entertaining) complements the adjacent living room, with the same pale palette and a dramatic antique French framed black-and-white wallpaper panel depicting a classical Roman scene. Neoclassical chairs with backs that offer a gracious, sweeping silhouette (but little comfort, except for a woman in a ball gown) bring movement and contrast to the room.

*Opposite and above:* Above the fireplace is a French plaster cartouche, circa 1850, depicting Greek mythological figures. The painting of two Korean sisters at left, above the sofa, is by Lordan Bunch. The designer added the new beveled mirrors on each side of the fireplace. He stripped the original mantel down to bare carved wood and left it natural. The sofa is a Diaz-Azcuy design, with silk damask over a stuffing of pure down. "To sit on it is pure heaven," says the designer. "It is like floating on a cloud." The club chairs, "Churchill" by Marco, were upholstered in a heavy-white-linen hopsack, soothed with down fill. A pair of gilded eighteenth-century Neapolitan chairs simply upholstered in white muslin with visible tacks (Gianni Versace had a matching pair in his Miami mansion) is juxtaposed with the frou-frou of white linen balloon shades. The pair of 1870s French trumeau mirrors adds a further note of embellishment, and their reflections bring light and extra dimension to the rooms.

*Above and opposite:* A gilded Austrian Biedermeier chandelier in the Gothic style hangs above a versatile pedestal dining table/desk designed by Diaz-Azcuy. The chairs are Italian neoclassical, circa 1860, from Ed Hardy San Francisco. They are upholstered in mismatched Fortuny patterns.

*Opposite and above:* The ten-by-twelve-foot study had no light, so it was glamorized into a media and cocktails room. The walls were upholstered in dark green raw silk from Silk Trading Co. The ceiling was painted in a gold-bordered swirling abstract mix of colors inspired by paintings of late-sixteenth-century Ve-

netian artists, including Titian. A pair of custom-designed sofas was upholstered in deep green linen velvet. The floor was stained ebony. A gilded chinoiserie cabinet conceals electronics.

*Left:* The sixteen-by-eighteen-foot bedroom, which overlooks a tranquil garden, is a rather grandly luxurious space, with the bed placed on one side to allow for a gracious seating area beside the windows. A series of neoclassical painted overdoors depicting the four seasons are a copy of 1745 sculptures by Edmé Bouchardon that ornament the grand Fontaine des Quatre Saisons on rue de Grenelle (adjacent to the Musée Maillol) in Paris. The biscuit-tufted headboard and bedskirt were crafted in gunmetal silk from Calvin. A pair of gilded George II chairs was acquired from Foster Gwin, San Francisco.

# Bush Street Residence

**A modest Victorian house, stripped of all turn-of-the-century nostalgia, became a modernist experiment and a source of great pleasure for the designer.**

In 1977 Orlando Diaz-Azcuy acquired his first residence, a quirky 1898 Victorian. It was a true fixer-upper in a transitional San Francisco neighborhood, which has recently been dubbed in real-estate lingo Lower Pacific Heights but at that time was sadly nameless and nowhere on a status map.

"I paid $83,000 for it in 1977 and sold it for $350,000 in 1990. It sold recently for $900,000, and at that price it is one of the least expensive houses in San Francisco," notes the designer.

The key to the design concept for the one-story residence, which was hidden behind a very lush garden, was to keep the essential framework of the Victorian architecture, but to simplify it, freshen it, and in effect leave the ghost of its former self, with walls as a palimpsest of its previous lives.

*Opposite:* The fireplace, with a green marble surround and a white Victorian mantel, was original to the house. The Brno chair was upholstered in purple mohair.

*Above:* An eighteenth-century Venetian canapé was acquired in New York and covered in a vivid yellow Calvin silk, with Scalamandre silk pillows. Windows, screened from view by surrounding shrubbery, were left uncovered.

"I opened the five rooms symmetrically and removed all interior doors so that rooms would flow, one into another," says the designer.

Diaz-Azcuy painted the interior walls a very high-gloss oil-based enamel in the palest celadon. "I left them bare, with no art, and bleached the floors," he says. "It was minimalist before minimalism. It was simple, very calm. I felt it had inner beauty. In the living room I mixed an eighteenth-century gilded Venetian sofa upholstered in gold silk and a pair of Brno chairs. I had a white Saarinen table, the first of many. In the dining room I had six Louix XV chairs, cheap copies, that I lacquered white, with white muslin seats. They were occasionally covered with a gold silk. When I punctuate interiors I use pieces that are very luxurious, or very pared down. I never go for the middle ground."

In 1978 the house was published in the *New York Times* Magazine by editor Suzanne Slesin under the title "Minimal Minimalism."

*Above and opposite:* A support wall in the study, with symmetrical niches formed with drywall, was designed to look like a freestanding bookcase. The Gae Aulenti marble table, for Knoll, currently resides in Diaz-Azcuy's Post Street office. The arch at the entrance defines the tiny five-foot-by-five-foot foyer. The enfilade of rooms includes the north-facing living room, the central dining room, and two bedrooms at the back of the house overlooking the garden.

# Sonoma County Country Retreat

**Orlando Diaz-Azcuy acquired a cottage as a weekend retreat, where he could work on projects while experiencing the pleasures of country life, just an hour from the city.**

After celebrating the first decade of his Grant Avenue atelier, Diaz-Azcuy decided that he wanted time away from the office on Fridays to mull over new projects, draw, experiment with furniture and fabric collections, and design and plan with objectivity and a sense of freedom.

He acquired a small and unprepossessing 1940s clapboard house on three private acres, basically in the middle of nowhere and certainly far from any fashionable watering holes. Privacy and peace were the goals, with perhaps a couple of friends coming up to visit for Saturday lunch and a walk in the garden, then precious solitude once more. There would be no social scene. A drive to the local bakery on Saturday morning would most likely be the only outing.

The house was beautifully sited among pine trees, with views of the surrounding countryside. Redwood trees formed a green frame around the cottage.

Diaz-Azcuy's plan of action for the cottage: visit, view and appraise the house, live in it for a few months, and then tear it down to create his ideal. But instead he started to

*Opposite:* Italian terra-cotta pots of agapanthus form a cheerful blue frame for drinks on the terrace. Groves of redwood around the perimeter of the property offer shelter from later afternoon winds. Two HBF chairs were slipcovered in natural cotton canvas.

*Following spread:* The sunny living room was decorated in a neutral palette of white and cream with a dash of terra-cotta, giving the garden views—and a changing retinue of McGuire rattan tables, antiques, and art—pride of place.

remodel and fix his fixer-upper, replacing floors, creating a proper kitchen, and adding new bathrooms. The decorating had to be right.

He added new white oak plank floors, which were covered in natural rush matting and sisal. Walls in the living room were painted off-white, and a red brick fireplace was also coated in a glossy white. The dining room was painted a rich terra-cotta tone. It was used only at night, in the glow

of candles, and was dressed with a funky-chic chandelier and antique French chairs, and later with Diaz-Azcuy's new designs for McGuire.

The bedrooms were poky, there was no doubt. He added French doors for access to the lawns and parterres. He painted walls in swags and stripes to create the look of a carefree tent in a Marie Antoinette dream.

"I never wanted to create a faux country look with

*Above and opposite:* Stripes in the hall and the bedrooms add a sense of architecture to the interiors—at little cost. Floors are oak, and all woodwork was painted glossy white. The small dining room is a tour de force of all-out theatricality, with a chandelier improvised from gilded wood discs and yards of crystal beads and drops. Diaz-Azcuy placed a Saarinen table with a marble top in the center of the room and surrounded it with his own rattan designs for McGuire. Walls were painted a matte terra-cotta, which was moody and atmospheric at night and in the late afternoon.

*Following spread:* A daybed was covered in natural cotton canvas, washed for softness. To open the cottage to the garden, Diaz-Azcuy added glass doors to each bedroom. On a bright Saturday morning, guests can watch deer calmly nibbling on the lawn, or hawks whirling overhead in search of lunch.

rustic furniture or peeling paint," says the designer. "That is not me. I'm an urban person, and even in the modest rooms I wanted a sophisticated and polished look."

The joys of bucolic weekends were played out. In the end, however, the city won out. Given the choice of attending the opera or symphony on a Friday night or heading up to his green acres, Diaz-Azcuy preferred the bright lights, big city. And the Friday retreats became a chore. He could easily make his city house the creative refuge—without the drive. Eventually he sold the cottage to a friend (who still owns it), and later he bought his St. Francis Wood house, which offered him the repose and peace he desired.

*Opposite and above:* Even in a small country cottage, Diaz-Azcuy loves a sense of luxury. A gilded architectural fragment, an antique Swedish table, and a plaster lamp (here with a Kraft paper shade) give the tiny room distinction. Sage green and cream stripes added detail and drama to the tiny cocoon.

*Following spread:* Terra-cotta urns and statuary give the garden a focal point and a sense of architecture.

P

eople think I never use color, but it isn't true. I love color! Sometimes it's very subtle, sometimes it's not. In Cuba, as a teenager, I once painted my family's living room shocking pink.
—Orlando Diaz-Azcuy

# Cosmopolitan Living
# Above the Coast

**Demonstrating his versatility and a finely attuned attention to clients' tastes and desires, Orlando Diaz-Azcuy designed a superbly polished house high above the Pacific Ocean.**

When trust, admiration, enthusiasm, and a lively dialogue are elements of a relationship between designer and client, the results are likely to thrill the client and encourage the designer to work at the very highest level.

Superb communication and a warm friendship between Orlando Diaz-Azcuy and his worldly clients made this California project go smoothly. Creativity and polish are everywhere evident, design is cohesive, and the outcome is luxurious in just the way the client prefers it.

"This was a dream house, and I am very pleased with every detail of the interior architecture and the decor," says the designer. "This is one of the few clients who understands the patina of age, and the beauty of antiques, textiles, and objects that show signs of time, and fine craftsmanship. They love accessories that are rusted, covered in moss. They totally understand that a new house benefits from a mix of venerable antiques and custom-made new pieces."

The longtime clients also wanted pieces from many

*Above:* In the entry foyer, Italian limestone gives a rich but understated effect. *Opposite:* A magnificent enclosed courtyard was created for entertaining even if the weather is inclement. Custom-made doors lead from the atrium to a croquet lawn, gardens, and a pool. Architects: Hornberger + Worstell, San Francisco.

*Opposite:* Family and guests gather in the living room every evening for drinks. Diaz-Azcuy designed the living room with five different seating areas to accommodate a cocktail party, a small group for afternoon tea, or just the couple, for after-dinner drinks. A grand piano, a writing table, a backgammon table, and corner banquettes add to the room's versatility. The thirty-by-thirty-foot carpet in an Aubusson weave is a splash of color in a room marked by restraint. The plan centers on an antique Majorcan table found in Palma. The curtains are tone-on-tone crewel-embroidered ivory linen. In an inspired move, Diaz-Azcuy selected a plaster chandelier, which is decorated in coquillage, a nod to the coastal location.

Two French art deco paintings were the first objects acquired for the house. The corner banquette and sofa were covered in Calvin off-white wool hopsack. Pillows were covered in vintage textiles.

cultures and eras in their interiors. The family is truly international, with houses in several countries and deep connections with a variety of cultures.

"When they acquired the site, I drove down to see it and knew this house would be quite remarkable," said the designer. "To follow strict local conservation codes, the house is sited in a very subtle way that works to its advantage. I always applaud limitation because it gives me great inspiration to work within those strictures."

The foundation of the house was set into the hillside, and materials and finishes were planned to be in total harmony with the landscape, with creeping ficus growing over the entire structure.

"We planned a house with architecture influenced by Mediterranean living, around a skylit courtyard," said the designer. San Francisco–based Hornberger + Worstell were the architects.

"It was designed to be open and casual but with a touch of formality to the rooms," says Diaz-Azcuy. "The family always has fascinating guests coming and going, so it is very comfortable and very much in their style.

"When we started looking, the wife would see something she liked, in Spain or Hong Kong, and we would buy it and find a place for it later," says Diaz-Azcuy, who traveled to Paris, Los Angeles, and London in search of treasures. When his client found an antique table or a

*Above and opposite:* A superb table designed by Axel Vervoordt was the original design from which later copies have been made. The top is a rare and unusual slab of lapis lazuli. The stone foot, a fragment from a Roman figure, was also from Axel Vervoordt. The Bösendorfer piano is a sculptural addition to the room, which includes a table by Karl Springer in the foreground and a French trumeau mirror.

*Opposite and above:* In the study/dining room adjacent to the living room, bookcases frame narrow windows that look down into the interior courtyard. The trio of moveable rattan tables in the center is by Diaz-Azcuy for McGuire. Pillows were covered in early-nineteenth-century Belgian tapestries. The Knole sofa is covered in wool and silk herringbone fabric.

decorative object, she would send the designer an image. He encouraged her to look at a broad variety of pieces, not all of them precious.

"I don't have an ego that demands that everything has to have my stamp on it," says Diaz-Azcuy. "However, I edited everything and made the final selections. The house looks like the owners, not me. That is just as it should be."

The decor is rich in history, with hand-woven carpets, contemporary art, antiquities, and custom designs that enliven the superb symmetry of the interior architecture.

A modern table by Axel Vervoordt, a chinoiserie secretary, a collection of antique tea caddies from London, and a pair of eighteenth-century paintings are among the surprises.

"This was one of the most satisfying projects I have ever worked on," says the designer. "The clients gave me the opportunity to consult on the total project, including the landscape, the schematics of the house, and all interiors, and to express my appreciation of a traditional vocabulary. My clients became real friends. I always look forward to visiting them there."

*Above and opposite:* This is an especially hospitable family home, with superbly arranged guest bedrooms outfitted with everything from luxurious toiletries to pens and CDs, books, international publications, and delicious bites. The walls were upholstered with a fern-print fabric from GP & J Baker. The same cotton dresses the windows. The Ironies bed is decorated with a soufflé of linen gauze.

*Opposite and above:* The exceptionally well-appointed bathrooms (his and hers) have understated celadon, beige, and ivory tones, and the subtle accent of mosaic floors and friezes. The marble-surround oval bath is adjacent to the meditation room overlooking the garden and the ocean. The Chinese daybed, originally in the Orlando Diaz-Azcuy Design Grant Avenue studio, was originally made for French export. The tufted upholstery and bolsters are in Calvin silk.

*Above and opposite:* For the "his" bathroom suite, Italian mosaic floors and ceiling friezes were crafted in a taupe and beige color selection. From the bath, views extend across the whirlpool bath past the terrace to views of the forest and the misty ocean. Taborets are ceramic.

# Sleek and Well-Defined in San Francisco

**A cosmopolitan classic overlooking the Pacific Ocean, this shingled house is a happy home for children, cousins, grandparents, and fortunate parents.**

On a hillside near St. Francis Wood in San Francisco, a house in the shingle style, built for a growing family, became the scene for aesthetic restraint.

Early-morning fog often surrounds the house, which was built in an elegant Georgian style. Orlando Diaz-Azcuy was particularly cognizant of the location, its microclimate, and the effect the dramatic coastal setting had on the interiors. The day may begin in the marine mist, but later in the afternoon bright light bounces off the ocean to the west.

"The house stands on a hill, and extremes of the environment here required carefully considered decoration so that the house would be warm, bright, and cozy on a cold, gray winter day, and calm and serene in October when the annual Indian summer can be quite warm," says the designer.

His program: a young, active family that has four small children and loves to entertain, wanted a lighthearted house that would be casual and modern, without pretension but with a mild air of formality. The architecture was by BAR Architects, a highly acclaimed firm based in San Francisco.

"The house is always full of friends and close family who live nearby," says Diaz-Azcuy. "Someone is always dropping in, and at any time of day there seems to be a lively celebration being planned. The dining room is the heart of the house."

To give the interiors a cohesive feeling, the designer selected rich but simple natural fabrics like linen, silk, and cotton, as well as chic but hard-wearing rush matting for the hardwood floors.

Diaz-Azcuy created sleek and well-defined interior architecture. "It is a truly grown-up house," he says "It will work well for the family as the children grow, and long after."

*Opposite:* Diaz-Azcuy found the Florentine baroque gilded mirror—a nod to the family's Italian heritage—in New York. It is the perfect counterpoint to the rather sober eighteenth-century Italian chest of drawers from Therien & Co., San Francisco. "The mirror dazzles, in contrast to the natural silk curtains and pale ivory tones of the room, which is really quite restrained," says the designer. The hardwood floor was covered in rush matting. Natural silk curtains hang from simple rods. Diaz-Azcuy does not generally believe in overly designed curtains.

*Previous spread:* The sixteen-by-thirty-two-foot living room is divided into two versatile seating areas. Adjacent to the fireplace, a pair of Knole sofas upholstered in natural linen offers repose and privacy. A coffered ceiling adds dimension and texture to the room. In the foreground, another seating group circles a handsome lacquer and bronze table from Therien & Co., San Francisco.

*Opposite and above:* Two layers of curtains—a linen gauze along the bay window and an overdrape of off-white silk—plus Conrad rattan shades, offer effective adjustments for light and temperature. The antique bargello textiles used for the floor pillows were selected at Kathleen Taylor/The Lotus Collection, a San Francisco gallery that specializes in rare textiles from around the world.

*Right:* The dining table, which can be extended to seat twenty guests, is surrounded by chairs in an ebony finish with red undertones. They were designed by Diaz-Azcuy and upholstered in leather. The blue-and-ivory oil painting is by Caio Fonseca, a friend of the family. Beveled mirror panels on three sides of the room were designed to increase the apparent size of the room and to add sparkle, magic, and movement day and night. The silver-leaf sconces, designed by Diaz-Azcuy, are from Boyd.

*Above:* Two freestanding white-lacquered columnar cabinets, which define the hall and dining room, are used as coat closets. Diaz-Azcuy designed them and had them mounted on casters so the dimensions of the dining room can be expanded into the hall.

*Following spread:* The family room/media room has storage for toys, a table for meals and games, and a highly sophisticated electronic system. Nine of Diaz-Azcuy's rattan tables for McGuire stand in front of the chenille sofas and can be moved to many configurations. The walls were laminated in two-inch limestone panels. Double doors lead to the family's gym.

# Edwardian Elegance in Pacific Heights

**San Francisco is a city of handsome historic houses with noble proportions and light-filled rooms. The project: Refresh but maintain a sense of tradition.**

For a longtime client, for whom he had designed downtown headquarters, Orlando Diaz-Azcuy took a classical approach to a city mansion.

"I am always pragmatic when I have my first meetings with a client," he says. "I always discuss the reality of what they want, and I talk about solutions and dreams as we are further into the project."

For this house, the plan was to update both the day-to-day rooms as well as the formal rooms. The living room, used mostly for entertaining, was enriched with large-scale contemporary paintings and simple but voluminous persimmon silk curtains that light up the room in the afternoon. "My clients wanted a sense of luxury, but nothing overdone," says the designer.

*Above and opposite:* The exterior of the house and grand interior stairway show their century-old lineage. Rich, gold-colored chenille sofas are dressed with Fortuny pillows in the sedate living room. A Harry Bertoia sculpture stands on a gilded, marble-topped Italian table.

# A Dash of Color in Atherton

**Orlando Diaz-Azcuy is known for his pure, white interiors. He's not averse to color, he insists. Just ask.**

For a young Finnish couple, a medical doctor and his business executive wife, and their children, Orlando Diaz-Azcuy made an elegant exception to his "all-white" or neutral palette.

"I love to work with color, and this was a fine opportunity," he says. "They had just acquired a developer house, typical of some neighborhoods in Silicon Valley, in a modified French Château style. But the architecture was hardly cohesive. It was not very French and hardly a château of any persuasion."

Looking to their Baltic heritage, his clients wanted an open, relaxed, and airy house for entertaining. It would be sophisticated and polished, with no fuss and minimal accessories, curtains, and embellishment.

"I listened closely to their ideas," says Orlando Diaz-Azcuy. "They wanted a house with a contemporary attitude—but no chrome or glass. They both liked the idea of a nod to tradition. It was a delicate balance."

As the project went forward, every piece of furniture was custom-crafted. "My clients were patrons of the San Francisco Museum of Modern Art and had already acquired a fine art collection, including a very coveted early Agnes Martin painting," notes the designer. Other trophies included an early Willem de Kooning oil painting and a series of Greek and Roman antiquities.

Taking a cue from neoclassical Swedish design and the colors of the Baltic region, Diaz-Azcuy selected shades of pale periwinkle, pale celadon, and a vivid cerulean blue, along with the contrast of gold and off-white. "I looked to a neoclassical Gustavian palace influence, not Scandinavian country houses," he says. "In the end the living room had just the relaxed elegance we wanted."

*Left and opposite:* A cast-concrete console table the color of pale limestone makes a superb stage for a fine Greek marble head, circa 200 BC, and a pair of carved and gilded wood finials from John Hobbs. The painting is by Agnes Martin, who wrote, "I can see humility, Delicate and white, It is satisfying, Just by itself." The two gilded "Chalice" sofas by HBF were upholstered in a vivid Fortuny fabric. The geometric carpet was designed by Diaz-Azcuy and crafted by V'soske.

*Opposite and above:* In the master suite, faux-marbled walls display plaster busts. The bas-relief shows a Greek mythological scene.

# Napa Valley Epiphany

**Under the thrall of historic Provençal archetypes, Orlando Diaz-Azcuy and architect Andrew Batey shaped a house for year-round pleasure.**

The Napa Valley has become a year-round destination for an international coterie of wine lovers, bons vivants, and escapees from San Francisco's fog. Among recent arrivals were a Chicago couple (and their beloved Portuguese water dogs) who loved the mellow weather, the proximity to the French Laundry restaurant, and the extraordinary farmers' markets, bakeries, casual restaurants, and small-town atmosphere of St. Helena.

The couple made a deliberate choice to acquire hillside land above the valley, just a few moments' drive from the winding Silverado Trail, but worlds apart. Several hills beyond the Chappellet vineyards, the thirty-acre property offers superbly framed views of Lake Hennessy.

They hired architect Andrew Batey and set off for an architectural study tour of the South of France. In St. Rémy they found a mason who would make their sinuous staircase. They viewed monasteries and Romanesque towers to find classic Provence's ancient history.

"Our clients appreciated the classic, iconic architecture

*Opposite and above:* The towerlike entrance to the house was built of locally quarried stone. The pair of oil jars was shipped back from Provence. The metal chairs are from Munder-Skiles. The house, with guest quarters and pool at left and the main house at right, has a commanding view of Lake Hennessy.

*Above and opposite:* The entry courtyard is sheltered by the bedroom wing, which has shuttered French doors in the Provençal manner. The new pool terrace and guesthouse were built adjacent to the main house.

as well as the materials and inherent simplicity of the interiors," says designer Greg Stewart, the ODA design associate who developed a close rapport with the couple.

"Our clients wanted an informal but elegant house with no country clichés," said Stewart. Floors throughout are limestone, and walls are integral-color plaster the shade of pale limestone.

Six years after completing the main residence, the couple decided to add a guesthouse with a pool and terrace. "My client also wanted more shade and shelter from the afternoon sun," said Stewart. "They like to entertain, so we planned a versatile terrace and kitchen for year-round use."

The guesthouse is casual, with a classic 1940s South of France feeling. In the sitting room, Stewart selected a custom-designed sleep sofa, a pair of Michael Taylor wicker tables, and Jean-Michel Frank–style plaster lamps. The desk chair is by T. H. Robsjohn-Gibbings. Curtains are simple Henry Calvin natural linen, and the Stark carpet is sisal with a leather binding.

On a Saturday afternoon in summer, light flickers through the pear trees, and shadows fall across the limestone terrace. "A feeling of calm comes over you," says Stewart. "It is a magic site, and now the pool terrace offers a new way to enjoy this setting and the views."

*Above and opposite:* The stairway is a pared-down modernist version of classic sculptural stairs in the South of France. The cast-bronze bust is French. In the living room, opposite, the antique limestone fireplace and trumeau were imported from Aix-en-Provence. Diaz-Azcuy kept the decor very understated, with a pair of metal tables supporting antique copper lamps, as well as relaxed linen-covered sofas and a pair of Michael Taylor leather-upholstered bergère chairs.

*Opposite:* An iron and rock crystal chandelier from Formations hangs above a custom-made walnut table from Dessin Fournir. The chairs, also by Dessin Fournir, have a custom gesso finish. Simple but lavish curtains were made of practical peach/beige polyester taffeta, unlined for lightness.

*Above:* The kitchen, a modern variation of traditional Provençal kitchens, has ebonized cabinets. Walls were covered in practical white ceramic tiles from Waterworks, and the countertops are of honed Carrara marble. The faucets are Harrington Brass in a satin nickel finish.

*Above and opposite:* A classic rococo Michael Taylor bed is dressed with a Fortuny cover and a Frette cashmere blanket. The gilded twig table is by Rose Tarlow Melrose House. With a view over the valley, the bath invites lingering. The surround is of honed Calacatta marble. Harrington Brass fittings were crafted in satin-finish nickel.

*Opposite and above:* The new guest-house was designed in the same modern Provençal style. Like the bedroom wing of the main house, it has painted steel doors and painted wood shutters for complete temperature and weather control. A pair of 1940s French chairs from Amy Perlin Antiques adds a casual note to the versatile room, which serves as both a weekend retreat and guest quarters. The custom sofa by Marco Fine Furniture is covered in Henry Calvin linen.

*Above and opposite:* A Michael Taylor table with a bleached-teak top is circled by Munder-Skiles chairs. The teak bar stools are from Sutherland. In the kitchen, steel-framed bifold windows open the room to the bar and terrace. A Viking barbecue grill/stove has a heavy-duty custom vent and hood.

*Following spread:* The new swimming pool, with views to the northern reaches of the Napa Valley, has Sutherland teak chaise longues, as well as Munder-Skiles sofas and tables in metal and teak. Callery pear trees were selected for their pure-white blossoms in spring, and their rich red and maroon autumn color.

# Russian Hill Reverie

**Sculptural furniture and contemporary art give a 1950s bay-view house a sense of stature and character.**

In San Francisco the desire for a view may trump the importance of good architecture. The Russian Hill house Orlando Diaz-Azcuy and his colleague Greg Stewart were commissioned to remodel dated from the 1950s. The original architecture of the five-thousand-square-foot house lacked distinction or historicism, and a series of remodels had left it a pastiche of ill-advised architectural oddments. Still, the view in all directions was stunning, even if the interiors were a mishmash.

"I had to pare down the interiors and create a unifying architectural element that would tie all the rooms together," says Diaz-Azcuy. Inspired by Frank Lloyd Wright, who understood the power of beautiful stone to add gravitas to interiors, he installed a limestone-clad wall that leads the eye from the entry up to the third floor.

*Opposite:* In a minimalist room, the silhouettes of furniture and the graphic punch of art become important. A series of "Egg" chairs by Arne Jacobsen (1958) surround a mahogany table with an ebony finish. The precise prints are from a series by Gary Stephan. The custom-designed banquette was covered in dark brown chenille.

*Opposite and above:* The dining room chairs are "Trent" by Kerry Joyce. A painting above the limestone shelf is by Richard Serra. The dining table was designed by Diaz-Azcuy, and two ivory-painted chairs are from the collection of Michael Taylor. A new limestone wall that rises from the entry to the living room is an important part of the remodel.

*Opposite and above:* Designer Greg Stewart designed an overscale tufted headboard in ivory Edelman leather to give the three-hundred-square-foot bedroom robust scale. Lamps are the Aida design by Diaz-Azcuy for Boyd.

*Above and opposite:* In the media room, a bar has nickel fittings and a travertine backsplash. Viewed from the house, the late-afternoon fog whips through the Golden Gate Bridge.

# In the California Wine Country

**Orlando Diaz-Azcuy designed rooms and terraces for summer repose within Robert Zinkhan's graphic Barragán-esque architecture.**

Sonoma Valley is less than an hour's drive from San Francisco, so it's an attractive area for weekend houses, especially for those who want to try their hand at growing grapes. It was there that a family, in love with Luis Barragán's bold and exciting architecture, built their weekend retreat. With its ocher exterior and three wings surrounding a patio courtyard and pool, the house provides a cool escape on summer weekends when the temperature may go as high as 100 degrees Fahrenheit.

"All of the walls are eighteen inches thick, so the house has a welcoming, massive feeling," says Diaz-Azcuy. "I like the way Robert Zinkhan adapted traditional Mexican architecture and Mayan influences in a contemporary version. The twenty-foot ceiling in the entry, minimal detailing, and the open floor plan make this a house of great power.

The entry to the Sonoma house has sunflower-yellow walls that direct the eye to a pool with a provocative sculpture.

*Previous spread, opposite and above:* The house was designed to offer shaded loggias and terraces with pool and hillside views. The owners of the house produce olive oil for their family, along with lemons, olives, and herbs, and acres of grapes. For the upper-level dining room, Diaz-Azcuy's HBF chairs were covered with practical cotton.

*Previous spread, above and opposite:* A daybed upholstered in raspberry-colored linen anchors the neutral-toned living room. A chenille-upholstered chair with an African-motif Fortuny pillow faces a crackle-finish table in bleached sycamore designed by Greg Stewart.

*Above and opposite:* Diaz-Azcuy's rattan chairs for McGuire were selected for the casual dining room. On the lower terrace beside the wine cellar, Diaz-Azcuy's teak "Portico" chairs from McGuire surround a teak dining table. From this spot, guests and family enjoy views over the Sonoma Valley. Architecture by Robert Zinkhan, Santa Rosa.

# Near the Golden Gate Bridge

**A Spanish Colonial–style house was updated and refreshed, with open rooms, versatile plans, and views of the bay from every room.**

When a cosmopolitan family with three young children moved to San Francisco from the East Coast, they acquired a 1920s Spanish Colonial–style house in Sea Cliff, overlooking the Pacific Ocean and the Marin Headlands.

Sea Cliff is a very low-key neighborhood of elegant houses to the west of downtown San Francisco. Its main attractions are the classic California Palace of the Legion of Honor art museum (built as a replica of the Paris landmark), Lincoln Park (for early morning walks), privacy, access to beaches, and dramatic views of the western reaches of San Francisco Bay.

In legend, Sea Cliff is always shrouded in fog. In reality, it is usually blissfully sunny there, as residents know all too well, with light and invigorating marine breezes.

A quick fix for the Spanish Colonial house, said designer Greg Stewart, involved simplifying the interiors and making the plan work for this active family of music lovers.

"The 1920s floor plan was a warren of tiny rooms," he says. "I opened them up and turned the dining room, living room, and a sitting room into one large, open space from which the panoramic views are visible."

*Opposite and above:* A series of Ingrid Donat bronze and rakes wood tables add a modern and practical note to the open-plan living room. A Richard Serra monoprint strikes a graphic note above the fireplace, and two eighteenth-century Spanish chairs with their original leather add a noble presence. Ceramic pots from the Chinese Warring States Period, are from Mark Richards, Los Angeles. The sofas were custom made by Marco Fine Furniture and upholstered in a fine ribbed cotton velvet from Henry Calvin.

*Above and opposite:* A reproduction table in the Italian style is circled by reproductions of a traditional Spanish country chairs with antiqued leather upholstery. The chandelier is from Amy Perlin Antiques, New York. The bar has a wall upholstered in Edelman leather, with a black banquette upholstered in a faux patent leather. In the monchromatic sitting area, a table by Jacques Adnet accompanies a custom sofa by Marco Fine Furniture.

# Perfectly All White

**San Francisco architect Andrew Skurman and his wife, sculptor Françoise Skurman, live in an ethereal apartment high above Nob Hill, with views of the Golden Gate Bridge. The white envelope was designed by Orlando Diaz-Azcuy more than a decade ago.**

Two years ago Andrew and Françoise Skurman received a phone call from their realtor to say that she had a new listing of a one-bedroom apartment on the seventeenth floor of a contemporary apartment building on Nob Hill.

"The moment I read the description—'all-white apartment'—and saw the pictures of the city panoramas, I knew it was an interior I had planned with Orlando Diaz-Azcuy twelve years earlier," says Andy. "I loved the apartment then, and it has retained its chic, sleek, timeless appeal."

For Diaz-Azcuy it had been a dream assignment. His then-client loved art deco decor. The interiors were minimal and pure. Walls were simple floating panels that were lacquered and highly polished in an elegant white. With no trim or baseboards to hide imperfections—and all-white floors that further emphasized their purity—the panels required the highest level of craftsmanship and multiple layers of paint. Craftsmen specialists required patience and the same zeal for perfection as the designer.

In contrast to the crisp white, one bathroom is finished in opulent gold leaf. The small elevator foyer has mirrored walls with backlit Lalique glass panels, and guests open mirrored entry doors with glass pulls also by Lalique. A fireplace was framed in polished silver.

*Above and opposite: A print, Bromphenol Blue–Cylene Cyanol Dye Solution, 2005, by Damien Hirst, hovers above a polished stainless-steel fireplace and a pair of Louis XV fauteuils refinished in silver leaf. The chairs were originally* heirlooms from Françoise Skurman's Paris family. The dining table which was custom-designed by Tom Dixon for the Skurmans. The white leather "Mars" chairs are by Konstantin Grcic, 2003.

Skurman, the head of his seventeen-year-old firm, Andrew Skurman Architects, had originally planned the interior architecture of the white apartment, removing walls and effacing doorways to elaborate an open plan. In a daring leap of imagination, Diaz-Azcuy and Skurman specified the Japanese white glass tile floors.

The apartment's minimalist approach is all the more surprising because Andy Skurman's architectural practice specializes in superbly detailed classical architecture.

After graduating with a degree in architecture from Cooper Union in New York, Andy apprenticed with I. M. Pei and Partners, and later worked in the San Francisco offices of Skidmore Owings & Merrill, and later as a studio director with Gensler, where he met Diaz-Azcuy. While he does modern, his inclination is toward the elegance of Europe and a sense of history.

"The moment we saw the apartment, we knew we had to have it," says Andy. "Orlando's work, more than a dozen years old, still looks startlingly fresh. His brilliant concept was to design highly reflective polished-steel window mullions (which seem to amplify the view and sunlight) and a glimpse of recessed polished steel where the baseboards or trim would be. We did not touch or change a thing."

Friends who come for cocktails are enchanted by the magical effect of shimmering glass floors and reflective walls framed with polished steel. To enhance the effect and emphasize views and lightness, floor-to-ceiling windows were finished with just a sliver of silken white curtains.

*Opposite and above: Venus Refuses the Apple,* a nude figure in plaster by Françoise Skurman, stands in the bedroom. The floor is Neoparium Japanese white glass by Nippon Electric Glass. The tall white rope chest is by Christian Astuguevieille, Paris.

For the Skurmans, the apartment continues to entrance. Early morning light tints the white walls in Pearlescent tones. Sunsets paint the rooms in a glow of rose pink. Later the lights of the city flicker far below, and the white apartment seems to float in the darkness.

Included in their museum-quality art collection are exquisite white plaster sculptures by Françoise, who has been studying for the last seven years with sculptor Mark Zjawinski at the Academy of Art University in San Francisco. Her refined technique requires long, exacting hours in the studio, working with a series of inspiring models, in the traditional manner.

"I am inspired by the work of Canova and Giacometti," she says. The white plaster works hark back to Italian classicism, but are totally at home in the modern rooms.

"We'll keep changing the art, so we never get bored," says Françoise. "We moved in and we've lived happily every after."

Opposite: Françoise and Andy Skurman juxtaposed the "Org" glass-topped coffee table by Fabio Novembre for Cappellini with a pair of Louis XV fauteuils reimagined with silver gilt by Rossi Antiques. The white plaster torchères are by Serge Roche, circa 1940. A Louis XVI recamier, an heirloom from her Parisian family, was restyled by Françoise with pale gray paint and white jacquard upholstery. Round console tables are from the estate of Gianni Versace.

*Above and opposite:* The Skurmans love the symmetry of pairs. Nineteenth-century Venetian mirrors, acquired in Paris, grace the walls of their bedroom. "Fresh Fat," an extruded plastic table by London designer Tom Dixon, stands beside their white leather "Odin" settee by Konstantin Grcic, 2005.

# Chapter Three
# New York

I am known for very polished interiors, but I personally appreciate eccentricity and the jolt of the unexpected.
—Orlando Diaz-Azcuy

# Views of Central Park

**A landmark building in Manhattan is the setting for a family's new duplex, complete with broad terraces, a yoga room, sunny views to the reservoir, and light glinting off skyscrapers.**

Panels of the same golden Indiana limestone that clads the Empire State Building, the Pentagon, and the National Cathedral create the rich facade of a new Manhattan apartment building by Robert A. M. Stern. The design and intricate stone detailing of the building hark back to the golden age of Park Avenue and Fifth Avenue buildings. The towering lobby is graced with more limestone, along with marble, quarter-sawn oak, and Venetian plaster.

It is here, with broad terraces opening to billowing green sycamores and oaks, that a family recently found a four-bedroom, floor-through duplex. They acquired the apartment raw—with concrete walls and the legally required rudimentary stairway. And they hired Orlando Diaz-Azcuy to shape the floor plan, detail the interior architecture, and design every inch.

*Opposite:* The husband and his wife, both involved in the arts, helped with the selection of every single piece of furniture in the apartment. A 1950s Ico and Luisa Parisi walnut chair from Karl Kemp, New York, stands before an Andy Warhol. It also frames a privileged view of Central Park and the East Side just beyond the broad terrace. The custom-made silk and wool carpet is from Rug & Kilim, New York. The custom-designed sofa was covered in pale gray silk velvet.

"From the start, my clients, who have an important art collection, told me that they wanted their apartment to feel like a home, not a gallery," says the designer. "They don't like clutter. They wanted no curtains or pattern, and total comfort with soft and informal fabrics and furniture. I call them Mr. and Mrs. Chenille."

His clients like to walk barefoot in every house—at the beach, in Colorado, and now in Manhattan. "They like to be able to open windows, to let in the fresh air," notes the designer.

The twenty-two-by-thirty-two-foot living room overlooks Central Park, with a ten-foot-wide terrace that wraps around two sides. The walls were finished in a subtle limestone-colored Venetian plaster.

"When we took possession of the apartment, we demolished interior walls and the stairway, down to the bare structure," says Diaz-Azcuy. "Robert Stern gave us beautifully proportioned rooms and a great layout, as well as elegantly proportioned windows. My work was to enhance the architecture but not embellish it or change it. I planned each room, but nothing was locked in. My clients are spontaneous, and they acquired more art was we moved forward."

Diaz-Azcuy designed the main rooms of the first floor with no doors and no closed-off areas. With five sets of French doors that are open to the park each morning, the rooms are light-filled. To balance the light and offer protection to the art, Diaz-Azcuy installed MechoShade solar shade systems, which are invisible when retracted.

"There is great luxury in the quality of the paintings and furniture, but the family lives very casually, with no rooms off-limits to the children," he says. "My clients like

*Above and opposite:* A bone-inlaid tabletop by Ironies was given a new base by Diaz-Azcuy. Four 1930s lounge chairs by La Maison Desny were upholstered in chocolate brown suede. A 1960s Merrow Associates chrome-base chaise longue was bought at auction and refurbished with gold-colored mohair from Joseph Noble. The two 1960s Karl Springer spherical lamps have shagreen shades. A Hiroshi Sugimoto framed image hangs on the wall. Beyond are the treetops of Central Park and New York skyscrapers.

The interior of the apartment was opened up so that from the dining room, guests would have clear views of Central Park and the East Side beyond. An expandable table in ebony and rosewood, custom-designed by Diaz-Azcuy, is surrounded by ebony-finish Patrick Naggar chairs from Ralph Pucci. The expressionist painting is by German artist Gerhard Richter. The 1925 bronze and alabaster chandelier by Albert Cheuret is from Jean Karajian Gallery, New York.

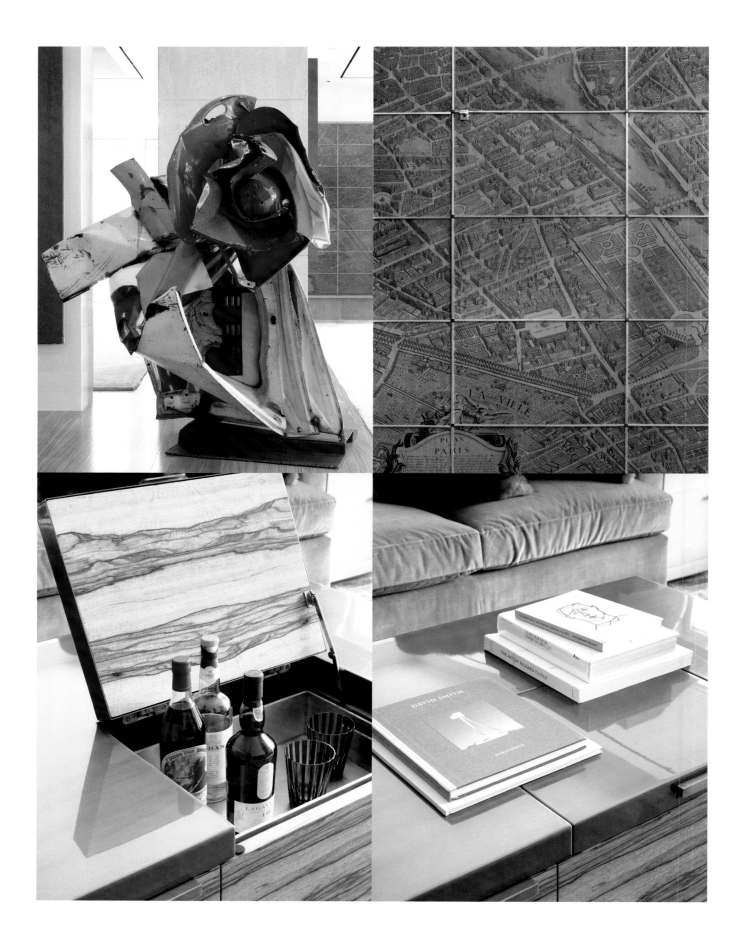

*Above:* The living room is a study in contrast with a 1962 car crash series sculpture by John Chamberlain in the foyer and the door of a 1960s Maxime Old cabinet with doors lacquered in a Plan de Turgot 1739 map of Paris. The coffee table/bar, designed by Diaz-Azcuy, was crafted with a lacquered bronze top and shows superb craftsmanship by Nicholas Mongiardo. *Opposite:* An early Roy Lichtenstein hangs above a collection of Chinese bronze vessels from C. J. Peters, New York.

*Opposite and above:* A dramatic stairway leads from the entrance foyer to the bedrooms and family rooms upstairs. A plaster column encircling the stairwell adds sculptural drama to the simple daily event of ascending and descending the stairs. The work at right is by Andy Warhol. The ceiling at the top of the stairs is lit by a LED light fixture that can be programmed for a variety of mood lighting. Most days it gives the impression of a skylight. The silk carpet is by Rug & Kilim, New York.

Above and opposite: The master suite has a wall of windows overlooking Central Park. The macassar ebony side table with ivory drawer handles from repurposed ivory piano keys was designed by Diaz-Azcuy. A silk taffeta bed cover adds a voluptuous splash of color on the bed, which has all-white Frette linens. The table lamp is by Nicholas Mongiardo. The enfilade of rooms leads from the bedroom to the bathroom to an office. Curtains are Christian Fischbacher velvet.

simplicity, and that was the direction I followed." There are no moldings, baseboards, detailing, or trim.

"It is extremely difficult to eliminate detail and maintain a sense of luxury and beauty," notes the designer. "The contractor said it was so refined that it was the most exacting project he had undertaken. With no trim or moldings, you can't hide anything. Everything had to be absolutely precise. It takes concern for the highest level of detailing to get this quality and finish. That kind of perfection may involve extra time, but this client wanted perfection. This is a client who expects and understands quality."

In the early morning, the apartment has an ethereal quality. It seems to float just above the trees. Diaz-Azcuy has achieved both minimalism and a sense of romanticism. When you are sitting in these rooms at certain times of day there is a a feeling of balance and calm that is sublime.

*Opposite and above:* A series of antique Chinese vessels sits on a console in the living room. A detail of the 1925 chandelier by Albert Cheuret shows the fine cast-bronze details of the heron figures and the alabaster shades.

# A Family House
# in East Hampton

**Orlando Diaz-Azcuy and architect Rick Cook perfected a modern family beach house that pays homage to coastal tradition in this elegant enclave.**

Hidden behind hedges at the end of a long lane stands a house with a commanding view of the Atlantic Ocean. While it is just a few moments' drive to the heart of East Hampton, it stands proudly between sheltering pines and a broad swath of sand, and feels completely removed from traffic and crowds.

Orlando Diaz-Azcuy worked closely with Richard A. Cook of the New York–based architecture firm Cook + Fox to fulfill a family's dream of a relaxed year-round house. "Rick and I—and the family—had a fantastic rapport regarding every aspect of the design and planning," says Diaz-Azcuy.

"The property originally included a turn-of-the-century beach house in the Arts & Crafts style, but the architecture and interior lacked distinction or function.

"For many practical considerations, the siting proved problematic, so the family decided to re-create the same silhouette with a new house," says the designer. "We would keep a similar style for the exterior but give the interior a distinctly modern approach."

The family desired an open floor plan with easy access to the garden, the yoga room, the infinity pool, and the deserted beach along the property line.

*Left:* Architect Richard A. Cook of Cook + Fox, New York, took his inspiration for the beach house from classic houses of East Hampton. Its roofline follows the windswept undulations of the dunes. At right is a structure that houses an ocean-view yoga studio upstairs. An office on the first level of the modernist building overlooks a reflecting pool.

A sixty-five-foot-long hall, measuring a grand eight feet wide, runs along the central spine of the house, from the breezeway entry to the kitchen and family room. The walls were covered with fluted wood panels in a pale gray tone. The hall makes a dramatic connection between the custom Cor-Ten steel fireplace in the living room and a lyrical Aristide Maillol bronze sculpture placed on a plinth in the reflecting pool in the distance.

This straightforward floor plan allows views of the beach from all rooms, giving a sense of easy-breezy seaside living that welcomes swimsuits and teenagers.

"It's a barefoot house—with the luxury of heated floors for wintertime," says Diaz-Azcuy. Windows on the ground floor are all free of window shades or curtains. Maple floors are bare—or soothed with silk and hemp rugs from Rug & Kilim, New York.

"My inspiration for colors was the early morning mist that surrounds the house," says Diaz-Azcuy. "The walls look white but they are a custom-mixed pale blue, which creates a more direct relationship with the sky and the water as it fades to the horizon."

*Previous spread:* Diaz-Azcuy aligned and simplified the interior architecture so that the emphasis is on sea views from every room, casual living, and a sense of light and air throughout the seasons. The living room, immediately accessible from the entry foyer, faces straight out to the ocean across the dunes. A Damien Hirst butterfly painting dominates one wall and seems to be a continuation of the blue-sky days outside. The chrome-based 1970s chaise longue by Merrow Associates was refurbished with a pale taupe leather upholstery. A table of petrified wood and a 1950s Danish ceramic sculpture by Axel Salto add texture to the pared-down décor. A focal point of the long central hall, above, is a bronze sculpture by Aristide Maillol. The silk and hemp carpet is from Rug & Kilim, New York.

*Left and above:* Diaz-Azcuy planned the first floor of the house so that the dining room would have a wall of windows overlooking the ocean and easy access to the terrace. The dining table is a custom work by Tucker Robbins, New York, with a mango wood top and both a sphere and an abstract cube base. "Ari" chairs were custom-designed by Diaz-Azcuy for the house. Crafted in cerused white maple, they have backs of faux shagreen leather and upholstery of off-white cut velvet by Rogers & Goffigon.

*Above:* A sculpture by Isamu Noguchi stands on a rusted steel plinth in the entry hall. *Opposite:* A pair of 1966 Swedish Arne Norell chairs and footstools, refurbished with the palest taupe leather, add their curves to the living room. A large-scale pair of chenille-upholstered sofas is placed beside a custom-crafted steel and cerused wood mantel and fireplace.

*Following spread:* From April to September, the family dines outdoors on an airy shaded deck overlooking the pool and the ocean. Sofas and chaises longues offer postprandial relaxation. A path leads through the dunes to the broad beach, which is almost always deserted, except for a few neighbors taking a twilight stroll.

# Chapter Four
# The Design Studios

Minimalism is an approach that results in great beauty and elegance, I believe. But while I can be perfectly happy in an all-white room with just a great chair or painting, most people can't live that way. Provocative conceptual art, found objects, garden flowers, fine old paintings, contemporary sculpture, well-edited collections, and of course a bookcase stacked with books, make a room come to life.

—Orlando Diaz-Azcuy

# Post Street Studio

**High above the bustle of downtown San Francisco, Diaz-Azcuy's newest studio is a serene and inspiring environment for creativity and new ideas.**

In 2001 Orlando Diaz-Azcuy Design Associates (with principals David Oldroyd and Greg Stewart) moved to a newly renovated office in downtown San Francisco, with jewelry shops such as Boucheron, fashion boutiques (Prada, Hermès), and Union Square nearby.

"There is no environment that represents me more than my offices," says Diaz-Azcuy. "I always thought I could live in any of them—happily."

The all-white atelier was designed as a laboratory for developing ideas. "The whole environment—including the lab coats my colleagues wear—is white, so your mind is clear," says Diaz-Azcuy. "Floors are pale oak planks, carpets are pale ivory, and I have selected objects—a few antiques and sculptures—to highlight. I did not want to present one style, one point of view. I want to accommodate all clients. Skidmore, Owings and Merrill did this years ago. The total concentration was on the projects, not the decor."

Light, from four sides of the building, controlled and filtered, is the driving force of the interiors.

"I always make the best of the architecture, without spending lavishly," says the designer. "I work to create a sense of luxury in the work environment, on a limited budget. My staff spend their days here, five or six days a week, so I want to create a comfortable, serene, and inspiring home for them, a sanctuary from downtown noise. I want them

*Opposite:* In the elevator foyer and entry to the atelier, somber dark green/gray walls form a dramatic background for a pair of dramatically lit English cut-stone garden figures from the 1800s. To the delight of FedEx delivery personnel and a motley crew of bicycle messengers who come and go hourly through this stage-set lobby, the office security system requires that they wait to be buzzed into the office, guaranteeing a brief and rather mysterious respite from the bright white daylight of the city outside. The figures, which stand on gray-painted plinths, formerly stood in Diaz-Azcuy's garden in San Francisco's St. Francis Wood. The white-framed mirrors that back the statues were formerly a feature of the Maiden Lane office.

to able to focus, and to put all their energy into creativity, without distraction."

All staff members wear a two-pocket white lab coat, custom-made in white twill and reordered at the end of each year. Diaz-Azcuy's coat, however, is custom-made with a mandarin collar.

"We work in an atelier, people of talent and discipline working together," he says. "It's a laboratory of design. We are serious. We are professional, not frivolous."

The interior design of the all-white rooms feels modern and fresh, but the firm is not pushing a style or one approach. Clients are energized by the all-white and rigorously uncompromising approach. "I am always battling design conservatism and clients' perpetual longing for the familiar," the designer says. "I like to stretch my clients as far as possible."

*Left and above:* An airy multipurpose conference room, opposite, serves as a practical place for new clients to meet around a Gae Aulenti marble table. Four tufted mohair chairs (a reworking of chairs from the Maiden Lane office) were designed to swivel. A white Parsons-style table serves for presentations or staff meetings and can quickly do duty for a light lunch with salads from Mocca on Maiden Lane. The rattan chairs, upholstered in chocolate brown linen velvet, were designed by Orlando Diaz-Azcuy for McGuire. Style signatures of the interior architecture: no moldings, no baseboards, subtle modulated light, linen curtains, and bare floors. "With no trim or embellishment, the plans pinned on the walls and the work at hand take prime position," says Diaz-Azcuy.

*Above and opposite:* An oil painting of two Korean sisters by Lordan Bunch hangs above an eighteenth-century altar table. The white ceramic sculpture is based on a Chinese design for a tulipiere. The floor is bleached oak. *Following spread:* In the reception area, where guests seldom linger, an early-twentieth-century Indonesian bench is paired with mixed-media metal panels by Tom Czarnopys. Glass-paneled doors to the conference room usually remain open but can close securely for privacy during client meetings. The white lacquer table was designed for HBF by Diaz-Azcuy. The English wing chair was upholstered in linen hopsack. Diaz-Azcuy also designed the striped carpet to emphasize the length and clarity of the long hall that leads to the atelier and drafting offices.

# Maiden Lane Studio

**With a masterful mix of antiques, art, and updated historic architecture, the Maiden Lane atelier felt more like an alluring townhouse than a design office.**

Orlando Diaz-Azcuy's Maiden Lane atelier was a homecoming for him. He worked there in the 1970s for the architectural offices of Leo A. Daly, when he reconfigured three late-nineteenth-century brick buildings into a cohesive office. The interior architecture was updated with all-white paint to create white cube rooms. Into the series of reception areas and conference rooms he introduced art, antiques, new furnishings, and white carpet.

"After working on commercial designs for many years, I wanted to express the idea here that a commercial space could have comfort, elegance, and a residential feeling, and that it could be personal and

*Above and right:* A large eighteenth-century French oil-on-canvas painted panel in the style of Watteau hangs in the main entry-level room. The sculpture is an eighteenth-century French wood and painted tole ornamental beehive. A pair of gold-leafed "Chalice" chairs by Orlando Diaz-Azcuy for HBF has been in production for twenty-four years. It was these elegant chairs, and his collection of eight stellar designs in the HBF collection, that kick-started his highly successful ventures in furniture design.

not generic," says the designer. It was a radical idea at the time, in 1990. To emphasize the concept he upholstered chairs in white linen and red silk.

"Luxury can be costly or very humble. For me luxury in an interior is represented by richness of detail and a feeling of history, perhaps just a suggestion," says the designer. "If it is too rich, too pretentious, I can't enjoy it. If it's too pared-down, it may be merely 'less is less.' A beautiful, comfortable chair is a great luxury."

In search of luxury, he asks himself, "Is it beautiful?"

"Luxury could be armfuls of spring blossoms. Fortuny.

Silk damask," he notes. "But I want to give a sense of modernity as well. I like traditional luxury materials used in a new way. It's definitely not two Barcelona chairs and 'goodbye.' Modern means a synthesis of design history. It's taking the best of traditional and the best of modern and making them both look new. Modern means avoiding fads, and not confusing design with fashion."

The best and most exciting design and art, with integrity, happens under the complete control of the artist or architect, says the designer. "One opinion is okay. Two opinions and it gets diluted. Three opinions and it's lost."

*Above and opposite:* The brass-studded leather screen, was originally designed by John McGuire, founder of McGuire, and made in the Philippines. The Chinese lacquered daybed was made in the late 1920s for French export trade and was upholstered in red silk from Calvin. The nineteenth-century neoclassical urn was an architectural fragment.

*Above and opposite:* The fourteen-by-forty-foot meeting room, which faced narrow Maiden Lane, had a series of overhead lights and white-painted brick walls to give the illusion of light. The tufted chairs were upholstered in coarse white linen. Diaz-Azcuy's sense of style, continuity, and practicality was demonstrated by this seating arrangement. The same chairs (later covered in taupe mohair) and Gae Aulenti table are now in the Post Street studio. A pair of white-framed mirrors at each side of the windows created an illusion of multiple panes of glass and even sunlight.

# Grant Avenue Studio

**For Orlando Diaz-Azcuy, the Grant Avenue atelier meant a new beginning. He would have the freedom to create his own furniture collections, to work on residential projects that intrigued him, and to express his passionate ideals.**

In 1982 Diaz-Azcuy was a principal at Gensler, already changing the way commercial spaces were designed. He is credited with introducing colors such as pink, mauve, violet, pale blue, and silver into commercial interiors—hotel lobbies, offices, a work environment—that had previously been designed with practical and hearty colors like brown,

gray, navy, or beige. Diaz-Azcuy believed that commercial spaces could be decorated with the broad range of beautiful, decorative colors and textiles that were used in residential interiors. In the early 1980s, this was radical.

He opened his own studio that year, specifically to design his own furniture collection without conflicting with his role as a Gensler director. He would remain at Gensler designing commercial spaces around the world and use his studio/retreat for a new collection for HBF.

Sleek and elegant, and owing more to Louis XVI than Marcel Breuer, the HBF line was an instant hit. His

*Opposite and above:* Even in the early 1980s, Diaz-Azcuy set up his office in an elegant residential style, with antiques, art, residential-style furniture, and soft, pale hues. For him it was an extension of his residence, where he would spend more waking hours each day than at home. He wanted it to be harmonious, beautiful, inspiring, and ever changing, with new art, armfuls of seasonal flow- ers, and a collection of chairs that would come and go. In the reception room, a gilded English mirror, an ivy topiary, and a linen-covered sofa bespeak a private house more than a hard-edged office space. A mirror above the sofa amplified the apparent size of the room. From the seventh floor, most of downtown San Francisco was visible.

"Chalice" chair, the "Governor" chair, and the "Havana" chair were in production for more than twenty-five years. He also introduced a new line of commercial textiles for HBF, once again in a range of rich colors.

"The success of my designs for HBF allowed me to leave Gensler to work in my own studio full time, and to hire office staff," recalls the designer.

Among his first hires were designers David Oldroyd and Greg Stewart, who are principals of the firm today and the future of the office.

The one-thousand-square-foot atelier, on the seventh floor of a downtown office building near the gates of Chinatown, consisted of a small foyer, a small office for Diaz-Azcuy, a reception room for meetings and lunches, and a large, light-filled design studio where his staff drew up every plan and elevation (this was in the days before CAD and computers). It was a calm, disciplined space, and designers were very productive with all the new clients who descended on this legendary chic space.

And yes, even then the staff—men and women, designers and associates—all worked in practical, anonymous white lab coats.

*Above and opposite:* To modify light at this elevation and obscure nearby walls, Diaz-Azcuy placed removable panels of white-lacquered plywood with a cutout treillage grid. He also added an architectural element to the otherwise simplified, all-white space. Crisp and unobtrusive storage has always been one of the designer's fortes. Note: Topiaries and silver trays for drinks are a typical Diaz-Azcuy design flourish, along with Tiffany drabware plates and Tiffany silver.

*Opposite and above:* In Diaz-Azcuy's miniscule six-by-seven-foot office, he nevertheless introduced exquisite paintings and antiques, and one of many Saarinen tables accompanied by his HBF chair upholstered in soft ivory leather. Displayed on the table and shelves were Japanese ceramics and sculptures from Japonesque. In the conference room, a quartet of ebony-stained HBF chairs contrasted with the painted panel in the style of Watteau. The stripes on the ivory and gray carpet were eighteen inches wide.

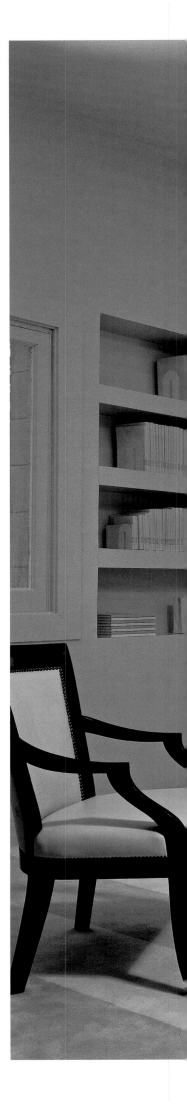

*Above and opposite:* An antique Chinese daybed made its first appearance, of many, in this Grant Avenue office. Here it was upholstered in beige Calvin linen with striped silk pillows. The chair is by HBF. The four "Chalice" chairs worked well for an impromptu meeting and could be placed around a table for a client meeting. At the time that he opened the office Diaz-Azcuy was just starting to collect art. His philosophy: It's worth waiting to get the best art and antiques. Don't fill in with mediocre pieces in the meantime.

*Opposite and above:* The Grant Avenue studio had ideal light for designers who were working at drafting boards all day. Diaz-Azcuy designed the open-plan desks so he could walk into the center to discuss aspects of the work. The interior was also designed for practical storage. Every surface was white. Visual serenity was the goal, along with superbly polished work.

# Chapter Five

# The Refinement of Design

I work in many shades of ivory and white and ecru and bone and off-white. If I am designing a room that will have a dash or splash of color, I'm happiest working with colors you can't exactly name—like a pale ocher, a translucent pale corn-flower blue, blush pink that is just beyond white, blue-gray the color of the Atlantic after a storm, or a faded Fortuny coral color, or an unusual lapis blue dashed with gold. A black wall can be very energizing to a room.

—Orlando Diaz-Azcuy

# Talking Design

**Diane Dorrans Saeks:** In your more than forty years in design, you have designed countless interiors around the world. Do you have a favorite?

**Orlando Diaz-Azcuy:** To my surprise, it's a baby's room for the daughter of a prominent San Francisco couple. I didn't know I could do it. The room was first wallpapered with clouds on a light blue sky. Little flowers and butterflies were embroidered onto a very sheer fabric that was draped and gathered over the wallpaper, then tied in the corners with pink silk ribbons. This was in 1978.

In 1980 I created a setting for a theater charity event in the Garden Courtyard of the Sheraton Palace Hotel in San Francisco. The tables and chairs were covered in gold lamé. Fourteen-foot-tall candelabras covered in gold lamé resembled Baroque carving. The spaces between the columns around the courtyard were draped in white gauze, which could be opened to allow people to enter and sit. It looked like a palatial eighteenth-century Russian room, made entirely out of fabric, as seen through the eyes of Deborah Turbeville.

*Opposite:* In his first New York apartment, ODA placed a series of blue-glass framed mirrors to add spatial drama to the entry and the living room. The white table is an original ODA design for McGuire. The all-white apartment, with views over the East River and the United Nations gardens, serves as both his residence and his office. *Above:* A custom-made long white lacquered desk in his St. Francisco Wood bedroom offers a stage for Italian antique art models, a protea flower in a clear glass column vase, and a stack of parchment-covered books.

**DDS:** You are admired for your modernist interiors—but you also create very beautiful opulent interiors. What are your underlying rules for design?

**ODA:** The style I create depends primarily on the client. We are more interested in simplicity, whether it is modern or traditional. Opulence comes with quality and a sense of luxury—no matter the style. We don't do reproductions of period styles. I always insist on authenticity.

**DDS:** When new clients approach you to design their interiors, how do you proceed?

**ODA:** Most potential clients have an idea of who we are, so I try to find out if that idea is correct. I prefer a conversation in which the clients talk about themselves, especially if they have children. A new environment always changes the behavior of the family, so I pose questions about the changes that decorating the house will create once it is finished. I try to stay away from discussions over budgets in the early stages. Although there are standard procedures to follow when executing a project, they are merely guidelines. Every project is different. The client's personality is the most important factor. They must be excited about the project. The budget is never a criterion to accept a commission. The client I prefer has a less formal attitude to life, and is not out to impress others.

**DDS:** You and your partners, Greg Stewart and David Oldroyd, insist on getting the architecture right before working on any decorating aspects. Why is this so important?

**ODA:** Correcting architectural mistakes through decoration alone rather than a thorough architectural renovation always ends up looking fake-. It is essential to get proportions, doors, window placement, fireplaces, and all the major elements of a room just right. With the right architecture, a coat of paint is sometimes enough.

We always encourage clients to put the money on finishes that truly belong to the architecture. For example, a sand-plaster finish in a traditional home can give you a tremendous sense of ambience and quality that is impossible to achieve with wallpaper.

**DDS:** One of the many reasons you are admired so much by other designers is that your work is never trendy, frivolous, or "fashionable." How do you accomplish this feat—fresh and current without following the moment's trends?

**ODA:** I am skeptical of trends in design and in any aspect of life. If a client wants something trendy, I always discuss the downside of the ephemeral quality of it. Trends are usually perpetrated by designers, antiques dealers, and companies like paint manufacturers or fabric designers with a product to sell. Interiors, colors, fabrics, and furniture must have longevity, inherent quality, timeless beauty, as well as classic lines and beautiful craftsmanship.

**DDS:** You are known as a modernist, but you regularly include fine antiques and art in your interiors. How and why do you use antiques in a modern interior?

**ODA:** I am interested in creating interiors that have life and reflect life. I don't like period rooms unless they are historic homes or in museums. The influence of different periods in objects, furniture, and artwork gives a house personality, but that cannot dominate the overall intention of the space. An expressive piece in a modern interior is not necessarily the most expensive. It can be a fragment of stone, a section of fabric, or a glass piece—something that is complementary to the client and the house. Antiques give a modern room texture, a sense of time passing, a sense of history. Art enlivens rooms, makes you think, makes you reflect on creativity and emotion. All of my own houses have had antiques and art that I've collected over several decades. I treasure these one-of-a-kind expressions of our culture, of our heritage.

**DDS:** You recently acquired an apartment in Miami. What is the design program there?

**ODA:** I intend to break the rule of Miami interiors. Being near the water doesn't mean you have to make a colorful plastic playground. The climate is the essence of the solution. I will be making extensive use of my McGuire furniture collection, combining natural materials with very contemporary metal and glass pieces. In contrast, the interiors for my New York apartment are a bit softer, more of a break from the hard edge of life and design in New York.

**DDS:** What new ODA furniture, fabric, or accessories collections will we be seeing in the future?

**ODA:** The offers are there, but I have not accepted any commissions of late. The workload in our office is constant, and I don't commit to new furniture collections unless I can have uninterrupted time. It's up to me. I will create new designs. They will have a point of view—and fulfill a need in a specific and very refined manner. That is how I approach design.

*Opposite:* A white lacquer table originally designed for HBF, has been a constant in Diaz-Azcuy's décor, transposing with ease from his Spanish Revival residence in St. Francis Wood to the low-key luxe of his atelier entry foyer.

The purity and peace of this all-white foyer seem to calm the demeanor of clients and FedEx personnel who traverse on their way to the design studio.

> " Mundane things enliven luxurious decor, just as quiet phrasing and bass notes add balance to coloratura opera scores. Decor should not be unremittingly rich. It's too much, and you don't see the beauty. In a room with museum-quality paintings or Greek antiquities, I may balance the luxury with simple white linen upholstery, bare floors, or discreet and worn Oriental silk carpets, and modern architecture. "

# The Importance of Books

Building a reliable and inspiring design library is essential.

It is important for a serious designer to read widely and voraciously on every topic—from environmental concerns and "green" design, to the history of art and design, the fundamentals of architecture, and even costume design and fashion. Interior designers must be aware of current trends in art and on the fashion runway—as well as popular culture, product design, restaurants, cuisine, travel, hotels, and textiles. It is essential to know about opera set design, new directions in international style, and even more basic facts about new products.

I always keep my design library up to date with a range of new books—on every style and approach to design and architecture. I am interested in the richness of English designer David Mlinaric's historically pure design and the rigorously spiritual architecture of Tadao Ando, as well as Venetian Baroque, Le Corbusier, Christian Liaigre, Belgian tapestries, Kyoto temples, and Hamptons beach houses.

Whenever I travel I stop to buy books at my favorite bookshops. In New York, I visit Rizzoli, as well as Archivia Books or Potterton Books. In Paris, Gallignani on the rue de Rivoli is a favorite stop. In London it's Hatchard's or Heywood Hill. In San Francisco, William Stout Books is an essential source for a wide range of authoritative books on architecture, landscape design, commercial and residential design, and the history of furniture or textiles. In my office, we use the Internet to research a broad range of books—and while I usually prefer to hunt through venerable bookshops for rare books, the Internet is incredibly efficient and we often discover quirky or basic finds to add to the library. I never know where I might find inspiration—perhaps in a biography, or even in a monograph of Lucien Freud or Valentino.

*Before Night Falls* by Reinaldo Arenas
A Cuban writer struggling with creativity and self-expression and all the changes that a revolution brings to people's lives. This is a story that applies to any society with ideological differences.

*The Decoration of Houses* by Edith Wharton and Ogden Codman Jr.
Originally published in 1902, this book offers a clear way to understand decoration, including superficial ornament that is totally independent of structure. It is an essential look at the aesthetic features that are part of the organization of the house, inside and out. The book clarifies strictly architectural principles and offers designers an insight into the enduring tenets of good design.

*How to be a Gentleman and As a Gentleman Would Say* by John Bridges
In a crude, rude society where good manners are almost obsolete, it is an easy, fun, and refreshing read, and a guide to social relationships. It is never too late to improve one's manners.

*Utz* by Bruce Chatwin
I am a serious collector, so I love reading about this passionate collector of porcelains. It's an elegantly ironic book that can be read merely for the pleasure of Chatwin's simple but vivid language, and then for the suspense of discovering what has become of Utz's fabulous collection.

"People think I never use color, but it isn't true. I love color! In Cuba, as a teenager, I once painted my parents' living room shocking pink. I spend hours working on color schemes. Many people are not attuned to tone-on-tone colors, or a carefully selected and calibrated collection of whites, and they don't notice subtlety. Soft, neutral, barely there colors are still colors. Some of our most exciting projects are true color inspiration."

*The Flaneur* by Edmund White
This collection of essays takes you into the heart of Paris. I have always been fascinated with the grandeur of Paris, as well as the intriguing back streets and the stories that lie within them. I believe Paris is the most emotionally fulfilling city in the world. This book should be read by young people going to Paris for the first time, and by old-timers so they can learn what they have missed when they have not expanded their horizons in the city.

*Too Much Is Never Enough* by Morris Lapidus
The most candid and unique story of an architect/designer recalling the realities of his professional life. His travails are very similar to what most designers experience in their professional lives, but most designers are too mundane or egotistical to let us know.

Lapidus understood modern architecture and incorporated his background as a decorator into his work. His words are inspirational for young designers.

*Yutaka Saito, Architect* by Hisao Kohyama
This is the most sophisticated, minimal expression of traditional Japanese architecture. The architect doesn't abandon his roots to create the crude concrete-block buildings that can be seen almost everywhere. He combines structure with art. His work is fully complete; his houses never need accessories to show how pleasant and exciting it is to live there. It is all about the human spirit.

*American Art Deco* by Alistair Duncan
A comprehensesive guide to what was great in the 1920s and '30s in America, this book also includes architecture, arts and crafts, jewelry, weaving, silversmiths, and glassware. This book makes clear how the same movement, using mainly the same materials, created expressions that were distinctly American, versus French, Viennese, or Italian.

*Axel Vervoordt: The Story of a Style* by Meredith Etherington-Smith
*Axel Vervoordt: Timeless Interiors* by Armelle Baron
Axel Vervoordt is one of the most influential designers/ antiques dealers in the world. Designers and antiques enthusiasts must visit the Vervoordt castle in Antwerp (by appointment) and the new Kanaal antiques and art gallery in the Belgian countryside to truly appreciate Axel Vervoordt, who has cultivated incredibly exquisite taste. Vervoordt demonstrates that good taste can apply to any period and any object. He is definitely one of the taste leaders of our times. These beautifully art-directed books are an introduction to a pilgrimage that any interior designer should make. The new Axel Vervoordt Kanaal gallery near Antwerp is like a fine museum where everything from Khmer statuary to Romanian painted country furniture and contemporary art are for sale.

*The Fountainhead* by Ayn Rand
A classic (and sometimes controversial) novel based on passion and lust but overall on the dreams of a purist dreamer/architect. A lesson for the young designer and anyone who aspires to do the best in his field. I believe that this book should be read by all designers from time to time to evaluate whether or not they have remained true to their dreams.

*Don't Sweat the Small Stuff…and It's All Small Stuff* by Richard Carlson
Major catastrophes make changes in our society that most of the time can and are taken care of by larger forces than our own. It is the small stuff that drives our behavior and our personality. As a designer, especially when practicing interior design, I find it is all small stuff. I have learned to give problems the proper time for their solutions and especially not to sweat it. Dramas come and go. Custom design is fraught with peril—and potential triumph. This books puts it into perspective.

*Plain and Simple* by Sue Bender
This quietly profound book is about the maximum power and fulfillment we can achieve through simplifying.

Any book on Luis Barragán, the Mexican architect. He is the master of bringing soul and humanity to the International Style. In Barragán's architecture, simplicity is both an expression and a force. Barragán never abandons texture, color, or craft, which nurture the most tender and fulfilling of human emotions.

*As you set out for Ithaka*
*hope your road is a long one,*
*full of adventure, full of discovery,*
*Laistrygonians, Cyclops,*
*angry Poseidon—don't be afraid of them:*
*you'll never find things like that on your way*
*as long as you keep your thoughts raised high.*
—C.P. Cavafy

Each book is a journey to Ithaka—Diane Dorrans Saeks

## ACKNOWLEDGMENTS

Books are a team effort. A wonderful and talented group worked on this beautiful book. It has been a pleasure to get inside the mind of Orlando Diaz-Azcuy, a man I admire for his talent, his fearless drive to create beauty, for his total focus on design, and for the triumph of his life in design.

Rizzoli publisher Charles Miers continues to have great enthusiasm for my book ideas. His guidance and insight are greatly valued. My editor Dung Ngo offers an insightful, wise, steady, witty, knowing, and objective viewpoint that is valuable and very much appreciated. It is always a great pleasure to work with Dung. Thanks also to Alexandra Tart for crisp editing.

This is my fifth book with art director Paul McKevitt and his team at Subtitle, New York. I have great respect for Paul's polished and graceful professionalism. Thank you, Paul.

Scott Cazet's meticulous work in collating materials for this book is sincerely appreciated.

**—Diane Dorrans Saeks**

To my mother and father, Hortensia Azcuy Garcia and Antonio Diaz Acosta. At 20 years of age I was given their blessings to look for the future and I never saw them again.

Arthur Gensler gave me the opportunity to shine. I appreciate all the clients who put their trust in me.

To the press, who encouraged me early on and stayed with me ever since.

To Villanova University Havana, for its support in such difficult times for all of us Cubans. The National Defense Student Loans made it economically easier for me. Catholic University of America embraced me on my arrival to this country. University of California at Berkeley's College of Environmental Design showed me what a university is all about.

My appreciation to Charles Miers and Dung Ngo at Rizzoli, for giving me an opportunity to bring my work to the public.

To Diane Dorrans Saeks, for her support during the last 25 years and for the splendid work she has done with this book.

My thanks to Scott Cazet, who has worked so diligently to assemble photography for the book.

To our staff, who rally around all the work we do. David T. Oldroyd and Greg Stewart have contributed for more than 20 years to the work you on these pages, and more, and their leadership is the future of our business.

To John G. Capo, my partner, for 43 years at my side.

**—Orlando Diaz-Azcuy**

First published in the United States of America in 2009 by
RIZZOLI INTERNATIONAL PUBLICATIONS, INC.
300 Park Avenue South
New York, NY 10010
www.rizzoliusa.com

ISBN-13: 978-0-8478-3076-3

© 2009 Orlando Diaz-Azcuy
© 2009 Rizzoli International Publications, Inc.
Texts © 2009 Diane Dorrans Saeks

Distributed to the U.S. trade by Random House, New York

Designed by Subtitle / Paul McKevitt

Printed and bound in Singapore

2009 2010 2011 2012 2013/ 10 9 8 7 6 5 4 3 2 1

## PHOTO CREDITS

Jaime Ardiles-Arce: 64-67; Langdon Clay: 6; Grey Crawford: 8, 114, 116, 118-123; John Hall: 32-39, 218; David Duncan Livingston: 15 upper left, lower left, 18-31, 44-45, 80-107, 138-149, 178-199, 221; Matthew Millman: 11, 41-43, 46-53, 110-113, 115, 117, 124-129, 162-177, 219; Laura Resen: 130-137; Lisa Romerein: 154-161; Jeremy Samuelson: 68-79; Tim Street-Porter: 4, 12, 15 upper right, lower right, 16, 108-109, 150-153, 216; John Vaughan: 2, 54-63 (Photographs by John Vaughan for *Architectural Digest*, Copyright © 1993 Conde Nast Publications, Reprinted by permission. All Rights Reserved. John Vaughan & Associates, 5242 Reedley Way, Castro Valley, CA 94546, 510.583.8075, maria@jvaughan.com); Toshi Yoshimi: 200-215.